THE
SOUL
SYSTEM OF
TAROT

The Soul System of Tarot

Austin Muhs

Copyright © 2016 by Austin Muhs

First available in this edition 2017

All rights reserved.

No part of this book may be reproduced in any form or by any electronic or mechanical means, including information storage and retrieval systems, without written permission from the publisher. You can contact the author at neonskyrecords@gmail.com.

www.astrologybyaustin.com

ISBN:9780986275876

Book design: Dean Fetzer, www.gunboss.com
Cover design: Carlo Armintia

Table of Contents

Why you should read this book!	i
Preface	v
Introduction	**1**
Before you Begin	1
A Word to the Wise	6
The Roots	11
The Teachers Before Our Time!	12
Chapter 1 – The Daily Draw Practice	**17**
Practice...Because Practice Makes Perfect!	17
Heed the Warnings of the Tarot!	19
Chapter 2 – The Calculations	**23**
Daily and Monthly Card Calculations!	23
Other Planning/Astrology systems I recommend include...	31
How to Calculate your Tarot/Saturn Cycles	32
Chapter 3 – Why bother with a spiritual/divination practice?	**37**
Chapter 4 – Procedural Advice On Doing Readings...	**43**
Why Less, Really is More!	44
Where to do a reading!	45
Chapter 5 – How to construct your Personal Tarot Chart	**49**
How to Determine Your Birth Year Card!	54
Calculating your Rising Sign Cards	60
Your Natal Court Cards	65
Your Hidden Potential/Vocation Card	70

Chapter 6 – Guide to your vocational potential card!	**73**
Suit of Wands	73
Suit of Cups	94
Suit of Swords	117
Suit of Disks	140
Chapter 7 – The 9 Card Spread	**167**
Your Permanent Archetypal Cards (Top Row)	170
The External Events/Circumstances Column	170
The Internal Development Column	172
The Hidden Developments Column	173
The Archetypal/Result Column	174
Chapter 8 – How to Use the Cards to tell a story	**179**
Miscellaneous advice on doing readings…	182
Which Tarot Deck Should I Use?	185
Watch out for Disreputable Readers!	187
Chapter 9 – Every New Beginning	**191**
About the Author	**195**

WHY YOU SHOULD READ THIS BOOK!

This book teaches you how to compile highly advanced and insightful readings for yourself and others. All you need to do is read the book's definitions and you will come away with a very real picture of where your life is now and what the future holds for you. This is a rarity in the Tarot world: most books take what is simple and easy and transform it into something difficult and hard. You are asked to master 10 different types of readings or you are given erroneous reference material that makes getting to the heart of the matter a convoluted process unless you are blessed with an extremely keen intuitive sense. That being said I have experienced incredible success utilizing my system in both my personal life and my life as a professional reader.

These modalities have given so much to my clientele that words fail to express its value. With a concerted effort, your actions transform into a magical process where you are actively working towards building a meaningful soul-inspired life, a life where you feel ready to embrace the unknown future without a sense of fear. Accompany me on this journey as the Tarot shows you how to create simple but profound meaning out of your life, while living in a world that day in and day out becomes more complex!

My new way is effective – it combines these esoteric systems with supremely helpful theologies from the past and places them into an easy to use self-administered format. To do a progressed chart properly you should seek an expert's aid. However, you can easily compile a basic chart without hiring an expert. Unlike my system, other systems give a client just one birth card. Personality changes when the progressed rising signs change. It stands to reason that if life's challenges vary from year to year why shouldn't your cyclical cards change as well? Later in the book I will investigate this subject more deeply. For now you will be taught how to understand the deeper psychological roots of the events happening in your life at this very moment.

And while identifying your vocational destination is vitally important it is also meaningless if you fail to find the source and your journey's true meaning. In order to truly and completely understand anything, you must understand its origins. This explains why the "meaning of life" has become such a hot topic in western philosophical culture. Many people search for it but it is never found unless you are open to a perpetual reorientation of your fixed perspectives. Meaning requires change, because how can the same fixed thing perpetually inspire us?

This is akin to a child really enjoying grilled cheese sandwiches and then continuing to consume only grilled cheese sandwiches into adulthood assuming that grilled cheese will continue to provide the same sense of euphoria. Obviously the child would be sickened at the mere thought of eating another grilled cheese sandwich. The concept that consistency and security will provide us with perpetual meaning is a blatant fallacy of human logic. Following this path, we just end up walling ourselves off from nature and the creativity that could truly serve to inspire us and take us to the next level of our human potential.

Why don't members of tribal cultures or civilizations worry about life's meaning? It's because they are busy living their meaning

The Soul System of Tarot

from day-to-day, ritualistically harmonizing with existence to the best of their ability. They lack the western sense of existential dread and depression that permeates our culture. I am not judging which is right and which is wrong, but I am saying that westerners have to try much harder and make a much more concerted effort to live spiritually focused lives in a modern climate of mass purposelessness. So many clients have come to me over the years wanting to know more about their true purpose, or the meaning behind the karmic/dharma cycles that are currently befuddling them. This book was written to help just such a spiritual seeker!

Within the text, I take a deep look at what time means to you. Great empowerment can be found when you refine your perceptions of time. Therefore, I consider it vitally important that I help you draft an understanding that first leads to acceptance of life as it is right now. Later, this leads to personal empowerment utilizing the mantra: "With enough patience, anything is possible!"

Cycles of time can either empower or belittle us depending on our internal disposition towards their presence in our life. Gratitude towards life in general is essential for success. I'm a firm believer that your worst day above ground is better than your best day below it! Obstacles or not, without striving to transcend life's limitations, we will not discover the great person we might someday become.

PREFACE

Time: The Wandering Teacher...

As far back as I can remember I have experienced time in such a way that it highlighted distinct cycles, cycles that are beautifully interwoven into the fabric of all human life. As a child every so often I would sense that one cycle of time had ended and another one was soon to begin. I had this odd feeling that there was some sort of strange inner clock ticking away, etching new experiences into my spirit with every passing revolution. Somehow this internal clock would signal me by presenting a different subconscious feeling that certain major shifts were about to take place. It was almost as though the air around me had changed molecular structure and was now composed of some alien element. These profoundly, unique, internal experiences are slippery subjects when an attempt is made to properly verbalize them. I guess I could equate it to when I was a child and awakened on Christmas or on my birthday. Something was different or special but I couldn't really explain it. I just knew that my excitement created some kind of special, different feeling that this was not an ordinary day. This is what I experienced, although more neutral in effect and not necessarily charged with euphoric emotion.

Being notified of these psychological changes can be extremely helpful in many ways. It didn't just help let me know that new things were on the horizon, it also allowed me to accept the fact that the past was gone forever. It's as if every so often, the universe would come and tap me on the shoulder, letting me know that I would never again be the same person, or feel the way I felt before. It's odd that these cycles were comforting to me even though I knew that I probably wouldn't be able to alter the effects these changes would have on my life. I would struggle with the emotional meaning. I'd often experience the strangest feeling – it was as if the universe was whispering these mysteries into my ear – as if life itself wanted me to be ok with the extraordinary amount of change that was about to pervade my entire being.

Since I had no way of completely understanding my feelings or why I was experiencing them, I kept these thoughts to myself. Maybe I thought that everyone had feelings like mine. Maybe it was just a nonverbal experience that needed to be kept a secret. Whatever the case I rationalized that everyone had similar experiences. However, to this day I have never questioned anyone about these internal happenings. Nor did I ever try to explain the experience. Instead, I just accepted it as a natural, psychological, life phenomenon.

In my early 20's I desperately tried to decode these mysterious happenings, but I never really understood them – until recently. I feel like so many of my early life experiences were a time-released form of spiritual medication. They give us a sneak preview but don't let us understand the real backstory until later. These mysterious life cycles are magical and hard to relate to unless they happen to you. The insane part is that I believe that everyone's human experience is inexorably unique. But then again perhaps no one else has experienced this unique phenomenon – it's really difficult to explain.

However defined, these cycle shifts led me to believe that my little existential taps on the shoulder would be meaningful to me at a

The Soul System of Tarot

later date. This perpetual change phenomenon was more noticeable to me because my childhood was filled with residential changes; we would move practically every year. No I wasn't an army brat, quite the contrary in fact. My mother and I were just a dynamic duo of modern-day Middle-Class apartment dwellers. We had been sucked into a lease and repeat mentality outside of suburban Dallas, Texas. This suburban apartmentopia compelled us to strive for an ever-greater slice of the American Middle Class dream, one kitchenette at a time. As a child, from where I was sitting, if I had seen one batch of linoleum I had seen them all! Point being, had I known about astrology at that time, I most likely would have been able to pinpoint these phase shifts on my chart in some meaningful way. Phase shifts only seemed to happen every six months or so.

I soon embraced the wonderful fact that anything in life can change at any moment – wonderful because it helped me embrace the notion that life presents us with risks. I learned that risk was necessary and needed to be taken, while learning what gambles needed to be avoided altogether. Later in life I realized that certain people chose to avoid all risk at all costs. I knew that a life full of intense change was just a part of my path. Seeing these tumultuous cycles of change firsthand also became a beneficial reference point for my divination practice, for only those who have seen uncertainty at it's worst can appreciate it at it's best. Making it through the dark tunnels can show you how those periods are simply trials and not necessarily overt threats. Lao Tzu said it best when he stated: "If I fear not death, what can harm me?" Death is normally looked upon as being the ultimate worst-case life scenario. However, if we can move beyond the fear of death then we can begin to embrace life in a revolutionary way that makes life much more exciting and wonderful.

It takes skill to conceptualize the truly infinite possibilities inherent within your own life and the lives of your clients. It also takes much courage, because looking into all possibilities also means looking into life's darker, more evil possibilities. Only a brave soul will look into the hells that exist on earth and the suffering brought to bear.

Obviously I am not proclaiming to have some absolute answer with regards to life's totality, but I can tell you that this adventure called life is a grander event than anything I could have conceptualized as a child. Frankly, I thought I would end up a working stiff with a 9-to-5 job and a wife and kids. (This couldn't be any further from my reality). Think about it…a guy from Dallas who grew up playing sports and eating BBQ, pursues Astrology and Tarot as a trade. It ended up being a vastly different career track than anything I had ever really planned, especially considering that I had almost no spiritual direction while growing up. Lord knows I couldn't make a decent living with Tarot in Dallas – everybody was busy worshiping football and pursuing other more pleasure-oriented lifestyles. My oddball vocational track doesn't really add up unless there is an understanding of the spiritual dimensions of existence. But obviously it was a part of my greater destiny that I ended up in Los Angeles, helping people to find themselves in a world that is lacking a spiritual signpost department.

Time to Wake Up!

Within my own life, I humbly believe that time works with such an uncanny clarity that I must honor it. Time is our teacher, whether we consciously acknowledge it or not; without it we are adrift in a

The Soul System of Tarot

sea of perpetually purposeless action. As anyone who works in a high-pressure industry will tell you, deadlines create results. Where do you think the term "dead-line" comes from? It derives from the term death itself of course. Which brings me to this conclusion: a healthy respect for death leads to a more inspired sense of life. Nothing brings life back to reality like a funeral. At a funeral there's no more time to take time for granted. You are experiencing a scenario where time has run out for a human being and this gives everyone else a reason to pause and evaluate his or her own relationship with time. You can then choose to explore what time means to you personally and how can you best utilize it for your own personal growth.

People do ritualistically honor time but only on special days. Take your birthday for instance, a true cause for celebration for anyone under thirty…I jest, but at the same time I feel like very few adults truly honor and respect their own birthdays. Think about it, how do most Americans celebrate? By drinking precipitously of course, celebrating the day of their birth by trying to forget the day of their birth! Perhaps the drinking is an attempt to forget about years past or is a way to avoid planning for the years ahead. It is sad that instead of enjoying a ritual based on an appreciation for life and goal setting, most people choose to get drunk and talk about the past. I am not negatively preaching against alcohol, but I am illustrating how in our culture, socially, we fail to analyze the larger context of time or the lack of meaningful time based rituals…And no I don't count punching the time clock at work as a meaningful ritual.

Sadly, in our society, time enslavement is an all too common phenomena. People might intend to set time aside for appreciating nature or to celebrate life with close friends. Yet, that being said, it is always a bit worrisome to me when clients have to be constantly surrounded by others. It points to the fact that they have yet to truly befriend their own internal sense of self on any meaningful level. Time is always open to being utilized however we see fit, sadly most people don't use their time on earth to its fullest.

The odd thing is, under its auspices, time will always allow people to enslave themselves. Father time must be kicking back and having a good chuckle at the masses false dictatorial characterization of his true nature. This is equivalent to a five-year-old yelling at his parents that: "there was no way these 'gross veggies' are getting eaten!" completely ignorant of the fact that the 'gross veggies' would be indeed be a much better choice. The child lacks perspective. Even though time gives us the freedom to do what we want, it is this same freedom that becomes the source of umpteen neurotic impulses. As Michael Tsarion points out, as wacky as it may sound, many people want to be freed from this freedom. They instead would like to have things all laid out, so that they never have to truly use their individualistic sense of will and can defer all important decisions to someone more "experienced" or "in charge" than they can be for themselves. This drives people to seek out false leaders, gods and prophets of all size and shape. If they lack a shelter to hide from trauma on the outside world, then the common folk will strive to build that shelter from reality inside their mind instead.

Science and common sense alike both point to the fact that people lacking purpose end up suffering from psychological problems. Without a true internally based sense of purpose, humankind becomes more machine-like than we would like to admit. The soul was not designed to be on autopilot and if people choose to operate that way the soul can rebel and start to cause

The Soul System of Tarot

problems for the person who tries to push themselves beyond the surface levels of existence. It's as if the ego has a built in, self-destruct mechanism designed to make one's life much more demanding unless one is constantly monitoring it. I constantly tell my clients, the ego is like a little kid nagging his parents to watch him jump off the diving board into the pool. Without constant neurotic attention, the ego starts throwing temper tantrums, which in turn causes us to act out in an attempt to give ego its kicks. In our own life we need to pay constant attention to these cycles in order to minimize any behavioral regression or spiritual back tracking. A Peter Pan 'I don't want to grow up' syndrome is common for the ego because it feels it's safer and easier not to change.

However one chooses to address their personal evolutionary process, it's high time we start to understand and become comfortable with the fact that time is our most precious resource. It means we are alive and spiritually challenged. Show me a man with nothing to do, and I will show you a man waiting for someone or something to come along and define his life for him. Everyone, deep down, wants a purpose. Good, bad or indifferent, everyone wants his or her life to be meaningful. The soul is not adept at being a passive life observer (unless exhaustive meditative rituals or heavy chemical sedation is involved). We should not take this for granted. The universe naturally wants us to create purpose and to thrive, but it's our responsibility to utilize this baseline creative energy that is so easily accessible!

This battle is not a simple straight-ahead fight however, as we have many different varietals of chimera to face along the way. The evil lurking within all of our souls is quite crafty and can be played upon in any number of ways. We should always be cognizant of our long-term task to decompress from the evil within, a process which carries much pain in tow.

Personally, I believe time is our primary teacher: it allows us a direct feedback loop for analyzing the results of our actions in the greater scheme of this karmic dimension. Some might even go as far to say that time is synonymous with God or Dao. What to do with it? How to manage it? Why does it exist? You could say that people treat their time like they treat their conception of God. Some hate their God/time while others embrace and try to live in highest accordance with their God/time. However one regards it, I feel that important distinctions can be made because time can be looked upon as existence itself. Without a playing field there is no game, right? All of these questions are actually an attempt to chain father time to our dogmas. As far as I can tell, time itself has no true agenda other than showing people how to embrace the changes it continually presents to us. Time is merely holding space for us to step into a more purposeful existence, although by no means does it guarantee us growth without effort. In simpler terms you could say that time merely represents the energetic battlefield in which we fight for our soul's development.

If nothing else, I think we can all agree that time is a punctual teacher! Time never lets us enjoy recess when it's time to hit the books: time is always running even when many are running away from it! Luckily for us, time also presents us with pathways to tune into its magical flow. How can anyone say that there is never enough time, when, as far as I can tell, time is all that there is in this dimension? The rest of our "reality" seems to be a hologram, as anyone cognizant of the quantum/alternative sciences will tell you. Lets face it, our world is paper thin and we know little if anything

THE SOUL SYSTEM OF TAROT

about time's origination in the cosmos. The staggering ignorance of our own field of play when it comes to life has caused a mass disorientation within humanity at large. Think about it, if you don't know what the playing field looks like, then you can't play a game correctly right? It's like a bunch of people who are dressed up to play football showing up on a basketball court. They wouldn't be able to play the game correctly because no one ever bothered to show them the fact that they were not on a football field at all. Instead they would have to come to the stark realization that their years of preparation in learning to play football had been in vain, as there was no real field around for which that old game could take place. Some of the more determined players might try to play football on a basketball court anyway, while others begin the arduous process of trying to learn how to play basketball years later. Knowing they had been fooled the first go around, inevitably made them stronger and more determined opponents on the field of battle. This is the choice I believe we all have in terms of time. Should we go on and try to play a false game that someone else has taught us, or do we reorient ourselves and learn to play the game by the true rules of the cosmos? This path requires humility and dedication, something that can be difficult for anyone to learn whether young or old. I guess there are still others who go off and try to create a game of their own, disregarding paths trodden before them. Anyway you look at it, the original prescription we have been sold with regards to living a "meaningful life" are usually a bill of goods, which we will have to supersede if we are to ever truly develop a profound relationship with our own conception of time.

Time is the Willy Wonka-like effervescent fizzy beverage of our dimension, slowly dragging us upward – only if we have the courage to break down the walls of our own perception. Time takes no prisoners and leaves no un-fought battles. It gives us the ammunition to take aim towards our internal adversaries and always leads us directly towards our next opponent. Time loves us dispassionately. To waste time, is to waste potential. It takes much divine energy to keep this vehicle running efficiently – to disregard it, as if it were beneath us would be a grave mistake. Time is a wind that blows upon us all. Time will never be experienced the same by any two people. Try to keep in mind that despite popular belief, we don't tell time…time tells us! The whole concept of "telling time" is really just another way the ego tricks itself into thinking that we have control over God, or over reality. When in fact we are just tracking our progress (or lack there of) with little digits on a watch. Obviously it's a necessity to have time, but it is not necessary or even possible to control time because no one controls time – only time.

As difficult as your life may or may not be, whatever your circumstances happen to be, you have earned them. So go ahead and get on with it. This dimension guarantees us that if we put in the hard work there are grander vistas of perception that we can achieve to that end. But slackers need not apply to this advanced program. If you don't believe it's possible to evolve, grow, learn, and enrich yourself, than you may as well put this book down and take a long nap! Upon waking from said nap, perhaps you could take Morpheus' advice from the Matrix and "Believe, whatever you want to believe," as nothing I am going to put forth in this text will interest you. And nor should it!

Time is too smart to exhaust itself on those who consciously choose to waste time. I am not being harsh, but I am firmly

The Soul System of Tarot

entrenched in reality and telling the obvious truth: time is a strict teacher and life does not offer many do-overs. I have half-heartedly committed myself to enough ventures to know that half-hearted approaches don't work. If you can't fully commit to yourself and your evolution, then what can you commit to?

Face it you're stuck here…I don't see any space ships beaming people out to some intergalactic utopia. So accept it, you will be here until your death or your transition into another dimension, like it or not! Existentially speaking there are just two options: either embrace life or renounce it. Either work your ass off willingly, which will eventually lead to sustainable happiness, or be dragged kicking and screaming towards whatever karmic grab bag fate has in store for you.

Time runs through us all like water runs through a faucet…if you tried to store all of the water that had ever flowed through your house, eventually you would flood your home, right? Seeing the fruitfulness of saving every drop why do we try to save every second of our lives like we are storing it up in an ethereal piggy bank? The first drop of water we encounter in our lives has just as much value as the last drop of water we will see in our lives. It is only our perception of that water that changes. As all water has the ability to facilitate life when consumed in moderation, water will also drown us when we are overloaded with it. When water sits still too long it stagnates and starts to attract fungus and other toxins. These toxins are representative of the backlog of emotions festering inside society, as water has always been linked with the emotions in the esoteric sense. Feng Shui practitioners and Tarot practitioners alike have known this fact for thousands of years. The thing is that all of this can be avoided with a little effort. The Tarot can help guide us by showing us how to avoid the buildup of emotional toxicity while helping us to channel our subconscious overflow.

Whatever you don't allow to flow through you, will eventually bottle up inside you, until your container runs out of room. At which point it will overflow and cause you distress of one sort or another. So in a sense you could view a fulfilled life like an empty container, perpetually fulfilled by the invisible spiritual ether. While many may be blind and say you have an empty container, you will know better. As Lao Tzu states in the *Tao Te Ching*, the usefulness of a house is the space created between the walls. The walls themselves are less than useful on their own. So trying to live your life with a permanent sense of emptiness might help you to understand life's true nature.

Everyone in western society strives to be "full" and to "have it all". But in fact, being too full should be something to cognitively avoid. When your life is too full it means that you are in an elevated position. When you are in an elevated position you then have much to lose. Would you rather be standing on the top limb of a tree for all people to see? Or would you enjoy the safety of having your feet planted solidly on terra firma? As a result, it would make sense that those who are empty at all times avoid presenting themselves as a suitable target for the forces of misfortune. There is no glory in becoming the scapegoat of an egoist form of fate. When you leave yourself open to be perpetually changed by the universe, spiritually speaking, you then have nothing to lose and can become personally unassailable.

With any luck we won't let the world bog us down with its unholy machinations and in turn we will float on, visiting the greater vistas of the cosmos. Don't get me wrong, earth can be a

The Soul System of Tarot

great place; yet only a fool would think this place was without great spiritual trials. Only the strongest of spiritual warriors will pass through this realm unscathed from the constant barrage of personal dehumanization present within this day and age.

Introduction

Before you Begin

From my many years experience working with and practicing the divination arts, I have learned that the "mystical" experiences of reality never really happen like they do in the textbooks. Sadly, even though thousands of mystics have talked about it, many people will live their entire lives without even examining this "mystical" state of existence. I can assure you that different life dimensions not only exist, but also are eternally present. At the bare minimum, I believe we are living in a world within a world, so to speak.

At this point it becomes a discussion of how much information can one person handle? Are you prepared to accept the idea that a different form of reality just may exist? If so, would you freak out if you were able to peer beyond that reality's curtain? Does this reality really represent a safe and secure environment? Or is the earth trying to tell us that we are strong and intelligent enough to change in order to vibrationally acclimate ourselves to other realities? Perhaps there are dimensions with only classical music, perhaps there are dimensions with only loving individuals and perhaps there are dimensions with darker tones than we see here. Would this be so hard to believe? Or are our imaginations so far gone that we are unable to fathom anything beyond the limiting sphere of the tangible?

Austin Muhs

If you look out amongst the general populace you can easily see how an overarching fear of the unknown has become the driving force behind our civilization. Most people are busy trying to wall off nature, living in little cement-filled, safety-sealed communities along with others who all compete to acquire more stuff or indulge themselves more than the next bloke. Emotionally toxic as they may be, these media materialists aren't really an overt threat, generally speaking, they are too busy indulging their own hedonistic tendencies to do much harm externally. Just don't get in the way of their ego need fulfillment and you should be fine.

Isn't it a bit odd that our modern lifestyles keep us cut off from any meaningful contact with nature or any of the perceived dangers of the natural world? Especially considering that nature is just an extension of our own consciousness. Wouldn't you think at some point people would have a desire to once again become participants of the earth and somehow learn from all of the other equally valid species on this planet in one form or another? Many of these modern safety-inspired happenings, arise from an internal fear of discovering the truth. Not many are willing to face nature, it requires us to perpetually labor toward our own personal growth. It's either that or we risk being caught up in a race towards our own death.

Despite man's best efforts to the contrary, earth is an inherently risky place. I imagine this reality makes many feel…uncomfortable, or at least a bit uneasy. People may say that our society's primary motivation is to acquire the latest convenience or indulge in any pastime that brings instant gratification, but I see it differently. I believe society's prime motivator is to find some way that would free an individual from the act of changing. The fear of changing is

The Soul System of Tarot

society's greatest fear. Even if people hate themselves, the ego somehow likes the familiarity of the person you are right now, as opposed to the person you might become.

Now don't get me wrong, not everyone, today, is corrupt or spiritually devoid. Obviously there are still other types (hopefully yourself included) who were born with a strong moral compass: people doing their best to live simpler lives despite today's complexities, people doing their best to raise solid families, people living by a code of ethics concerning treatment of their fellow man. Sadly, though, many of these good, strong people still avoid reality's deeper questions. When you are worried about putting food on the table there is no time left over to analyze why everything fell into this state of spiritual and psychological decay. Those who do have time for quests for truth might fear what they find inside their soul. It's simple to label the world as a toxic and evil place, it's not so simple when you come to the realization that some of that evil also lives within you – now that's a sobering thought. I thought we were born perfect. I thought I just needed to believe in love and light, and positive thinking, and everything would be ok. No, those are just lies you have been sold to shield you from the truth of yourself. Whatever you did to end up in your life position you earned it. Most likely you possess some previous karma or internal evil to work out or else you would not be in the position you currently find yourself.

However you choose to look at our society and how we have ended in our life situation, we should relish the fact that our fate is not sealed. Within life, the universe gives many opportunities to switch off the karma and turn on the dharma guaranteeing that you will at least get a few chances to step up to the plate. In short everyone is given opportunities to live a prosperous and spiritually balanced life, despite any hardships that may present themselves at various phases. Doing the right thing can be difficult, but it always brings internal satisfaction and long-term happiness. That's is the simplest recipe I can think of when defining how to live a virtuous life. For those who want to apply themselves and evolve past life's day-to-day drama you will eventually attain greater things. From what I have seen we can avoid the worst parts of our fate, by sharing the best of our spiritual talents, thereby bringing harmony to the world.

Correct usage of the divination arts provides a reliable vehicle carrying us on a path to bridge the dharma/karmic gap and make profound progress toward acting harmoniously with the rest of the cosmos. Becoming a master of your own destiny is no small task. But it starts when you learn to accept the cycles of change, gain and loss so prevalent in this life. We must summon the courage to view this thinly veiled reality on it's own terms.

This process of opening up to other dimensions of life comes at a price. Discipline and sacrifice is the currency. However, discipline and sacrifice are two traits that western society has trained us to avoid at all costs and yet they are precisely the type of metaphysical principles that the hermetic arts are trying to bring our attention back to. If we are unable to live a principled existence in this world, then how do we ever hope to evolve past this beautiful little blue planet known as earth? How could you expect to enter some higher spiritual plane when you possess the consciousness level of the average Joe citizen? That would be the equivalent of letting a violent criminal into a mansion full of fine art. Hence we are stuck here on earth much the same way a five-year-old is locked out of the liquor

The Soul System of Tarot

cabinet. I feel like if we were somehow able to get into another dimension, we would probably hurt ourselves or do something incredibly stupid. I, for one, know that there are bigger fish to fry out there in the universe and, if able, I would like to experience grander spiritual vistas someday. The Tao Te Ching weighs in on the subject in the following manner…

> *The wise student hears of the Tao and practices it diligently.*
>
> *The average student hears of the Tao and gives it thought now and again.*
>
> *The foolish student hears of the Tao and laughs aloud.*
>
> *If there were no laughter, the Tao would not be what it is.*
>
> *Tao Te Ching - Lao Tzu - chapter 41*

When considering your own quest towards individualistic evolution, I think it's important to remember that the external world is a fluid thing. As such, it would serve us well to model ourselves after that fluidity. If we can model ourselves after this amorphous perpetual flow within our own lives, then we may be able to become natural conduits for the life force itself. This to me is the ultimate inspiration for living a spiritual life. I feel as though the universe offers perpetual happiness for those willing to endure the pain of perpetual change. Whether we can accept it or not, I feel as though the entirety of life is a process designed to force us beyond our own comfort zones and into our own highest potential states of being. So buckle up there, buckaroos, because as you embrace the messages of the Tarot, you are also setting yourself up for a ride on a spiritual bucking bronco.

A Word to the Wise

Before you begin a daily/weekly/monthly personal Tarot practice, I would offer a word of caution. Once you open the doors of personal self-discovery, sometimes, or dare I say most of the time, there is no real way to turn back. What do I mean by this? The answer is this: the second you started reading this book, you consciously or subconsciously, agreed to embark upon a path of personal evolution; a path riddled with unexpected challenges and trials. Anyone who has travelled or is travelling the regimented, arduous path that defines a spiritual journey will lend credence to my statement. Strictly speaking, this is a march down a path that will force you to contend with reality's darker sides. At a bare minimum, you can expect to duel with your own shadow side – a duel where only one true victor emerges.

When you battle with your dark side there is no guarantee that you will win. You may want to quit or turn back to your old ways. To which I say you should let go of fear and embrace change with both arms. Lao Tzu's words need to be repeated: "If I fear not death, what can harm me?" I feel that everyone should study this empowering statement. It bears repeating: if he wasn't afraid of death then anything was possible.

Although I have warned against reading for others as a profession, I know some will be bound and determined to follow this path no matter what. If you embark upon the quest of reading for others, be prepared for a massive energy drain. You will need a

THE SOUL SYSTEM OF TAROT

network of healers or other like-minded confederates who you can call upon in an emergency. I'm not talking about imagining yourself bathed in white light before and after a reading. That's just new age nonsense! It's weak and useless. It's like going against the US army with a pitchfork and a paper shield…you may as well stay at home and beat yourself up if you think that's a viable plan.

The problem is easily defined: people often get brainwashed into believing that evil isn't powerful. Well I'm here to blast that lie into oblivion. Evil is extremely powerful, if evil was easily defeated we would all be able to easily progress into a spiritually harmonious state of being. Evil is maniacally treacherous. We have to go through hell in order to regain our spiritual sanity on this plane of existence. When we start unlocking our psychic abilities we fall into the trap of believing we have "superhuman powers." This is just your ego taking you for a ride. You are a leaf trembling in the wind, its not until you have endured decades of spiritual shielding (which comes from training and good karma) that you will be skillful enough to resist evil's magnetic pull. Until then you had better work on letting go of fear and prepare yourself for wave after wave of vicious underhanded assaults. Evil will attack you psychologically, until it realizes that this isn't working. At this point you may actually encounter some enemies in the flesh and then you may have to defend yourself. Self-defense is the true key to any good offense. If you can't defend yourself then don't expect anyone to rally behind you.

When you conduct readings for others you are opening yourself up to their subconscious energy field, a phenomena which represents a bit of a Pandora's box scenario. In essence you are lowering the drawbridge and you are willingly letting whoever is behind the gate's other side into your headspace. To say the least, this causes problems, especially when dealing with energy vampires.

This line of work is spiritually, psychologically and physically dangerous unless you are completely dedicated to spiritual cleansing in any of its workable forms. You can contract a client's illness. You can absorb a client's bad habits and clients can steal your energy. If you are not prepared to deal with these issues, then look for another vocation. In order to experience success, a reader needs a support network of healers and guides. A healing support network or a way to heal yourself is mandatory because you will be sailing into very hellish psychological waters. However, doing readings for yourself is totally safe. No harm will ever come to you if you just use this information for your own purposes.

I personally wish that I had been enlightened on the perils that I was likely to face in this profession. I went in to it believing that I would have a better career if I were doing what I love to do. I quickly learned that no great vocational path is without great challenges. But then this leads me to one of my other favorite quotes: "I have never begun any true adventure for which I was adequately prepared." I hope by now you are convinced that readings for others is a difficult trade to practice safely. Again, in my experience when you are just doing it for yourself you will have zero problems, unless you are doing black magic or something stupid alongside it.

Doing readings is like opening a door: 95 times out of 100 you know ahead of time where an open door will lead you. However, occasionally you open a door and out pops something completely unexpected. This can happen during readings as well. Believe me, many people, roughly 30-40 percent, are very psychologically toxic. You are open to unwittingly taking on their bad mojo. This is a real problem especially if you lack the knowledge as to how to cleanse yourself after facing these psychologically disquieting energies. Believe me, the meager cash payout is not worth the physical/psychological anguish that you will experience. This type of work is done from the heart and not for the cash. Money is necessary to exist, but if you are doing this trade purely for monetary gain then find another. This vocation is not for you. Resist any codependent urges to play hero and "fix" other people. It's a fool's quest to try and heal the world unless you have solid grasp on your own healing process. If you are still in the grips of your neurotic obsessions, advising others on how to overcome their problems becomes a blind-leading-the-blind exercise. Would you trust a morbidly obese doctor offering a weight loss treatment? If so, then I have an acre of ocean front property for sale in the Mohave Desert.

In ages past, only those within society's spiritual caste or those who were full time healers or monks etc. practiced divination, people who were well trained to deal with the inherent evils of the trade. If you want to see the end result of doing this practice in an unsafe way, just go and visit your local psychic reading shop. Usually the people doing the readings are almost always overweight. This results from a combination of personal greed coupled with absorbing other people's energies and failing to cleanse in any meaningful way. Most shop readers also look physically distraught. My heart truly goes out to these psychics – I believe that they are grossly unaware of the danger that they face. Even though most of them I have encountered are morally questionable (a subject I touch on later) I am sure that talented shop readers exist somewhere. Always look for online reviews, if you for some reason feel compelled to try one of these places out (something I don't recommend).

Austin Muhs

When in doubt, consult someone such as myself for advice on what to expect. At the end of the day, if you are only reading for yourself you will be able to maintain a much safer energetic disposition. Your readings will also still help you to make vastly more spiritual progress than the average Joe, enabling you to tap into the innate wisdom of your own higher self. This will help you do great things for others in the external world, the first of which is generally establishing firm boundaries around which persons you will and will not help. Remember you should only work to help those who are willing to help themselves. Pay attention to those in society with innate talents who could possess the ability to help many in the external world.

However these spiritual changes manifest in your life, I can assure you that with effort and personal commitment towards evolution, these modalities can bring drastic life changes and reformations. The key is to look at the cards objectively and listen to the messages they are trying to pass. Reject any egocentric need to be right about your own life.

One card in different situational circumstances can mean many different things. I constantly find myself pulling together different meanings of readings after the fact. I usually will text or email these after-the-fact insights to my clients as I feel that additional information is always valuable when building client trust. If you forgot something during the reading, be honest and let them know you forgot. There is no harm in being human, but there is harm when you are not giving your clients 110 percent of your effort.

One of my biggest karmic errors took place early on in my career. I would occasionally advise people to get divorced when it appeared that the love in their relationship had died. I failed to

The Soul System of Tarot

understand at the time, the true karmic ramifications of a divorce. Divorce rips people and families apart. Unless there is physical violence or other extreme circumstance then the couple really should try and work out their problems. There is deeply rooted karma within marriage and the metaphysical texts talk about having to reincarnate again to balance out the karma from previous unfinished marriages. So how would you like to die only to find out that you have to go back and get married again to an ex that you divorced? Sounds like a nightmare eh? As so often happens in life it comes down to a pay now or pay later scenario.

The Roots

Why are these ancient arts so truthful and effective? Astrology, Tarot and Numerology were the meaningful equivalent of ancient psychology/philosophy. Over the years these arts have been purposely watered/dumbed down by the powers that be. In some cases the general populace equates these studies to little more than superstitions for idiots. Heaven forbid you look outside the scientific or dogmatic monotheistic paradigms in your search for meaningful life answers. There is no hiding the fact that had the church not excommunicated these meaningful tools of self-healing from the world, we would have no need to reach out to earthly religious leaders for guidance. The Tarot is the most cost effective spiritual psychologist you will ever find.

Without using these hermetic arts as a spiritual crutch, I know that my path would have been much more difficult over the past five to seven years. The Tarot has made my life better and along with my other spiritual practices, given me a sense of clarity I never thought possible. I feel as though the re-emergence of these arts in a meaningful format is a major key in restoring the self-healing processes of the human race. To safely navigate the world's perils, a human needs friends. The Tarot can be your friend, comforting you through tough times. The beautiful part about the Tarot – it requires nothing from you but an open mind regarding your own honest self-assessment.

The Teachers Before Our Time!

Rest easy, knowing that many human beings have been able to transcend life's trials and make it out of this dimension and advance on to find grander spiritual vistas (move over Jesus, you've got company). If you decide at some point that you want to investigate life in other (less problematic) dimensions of the universe, then developing a dedicated methodology towards personal evolution may prove quite handy. There are no shortcuts on this path. You will have to struggle mightily for your freedom. This world presents us with traps in every form and fashion, all in an effort to keep us chained to lower versions of ourselves. Hell is apparently experiencing a soul shortage and is trying to recruit as many people as possible for this upcoming millennium. This is why spiritual practices were developed, to help shield spiritual adepts from negative influences and to shed toxic energies in as expedient a manner as possible.

Practicing the Tarot is a form of training wheels for psychic development. The wonderful thing is that you don't need to know how to use your intuitive skills to do a great reading, the cards will do the heavy psychic lifting for you. The intuitive element comes

THE SOUL SYSTEM OF TAROT

into play when you are shuffling the cards and picking them while they are face down. (After you set your intention and ask your question of course.) The cards were composed to be a true living oracle so they know what to do on their own, you don't ever have to babysit or direct them. All the cards require in return for their service is your trust and respect. Everything in the universe, animate or otherwise, has some form of value and the Tarot represents thousands of years of ancestral wisdom. As Michael Tsarion points out in his Irish Origins of Civilization series, the word Torah actually comes from the root word "Tarot". Which comes from the word "Tarut" which is where we derive the modern day version of the word "Truth." This illustrates just how vital this tool of divination was to people in times past.

When utilizing Mr. Tsarion's *The Path of the Fool* companion book as an auxiliary reference work, it is very possible to do readings with little more than a question and an ability to read the definitions as you go. Down the line you may start to get visions of people. You may begin to spew out intuitive insights, (if you are doing readings for others that is) but how exactly this all takes place is anyone's guess. I have a vague inkling as to how psychic phenomena takes place but the exact mechanics behind the Tarot is still a bit of a mystery to me. Everyone will have his or her own unique experiences in this regard, so I don't want to say too much. Just go with your own unique flow and remember to practice, practice, practice! In the beginning memorization is the absolute key to a good fluid reading, so studying Mr. Tsarion's definitions in depth is essential!

We must always retain a reverence for the wisdom of the Tarot, as it doesn't just bestow its deeper guidance upon everyone. It requires a patient and benevolently minded inquirer to tap into the deepest level of the Tarot's teachings. I feel that many spiritual masters relied upon these divination arts in times past as a way to visually teach others the outcomes of their current life path. They were then able to simultaneously give advice on how to change course if the spiritual path needed to be altered. Remember, for as long as you exist, danger will be an ever-present issue. Whether that danger is internal or external, it is something that needs to be guarded against. Life is inherently risky – death is always riding shotgun right along side of life.

Before we can truly respect life and all the opportunities it brings us, we must first garner a true respect for death. I believe, in their own unique way, everyone respects death. To ignore its presence forces us into a limited worldview. Death is not always a bad thing. Many times it is the greatest teacher human beings will encounter during their lives. It comes in many forms: psychological death, spiritual death and physical death, each one as valuable as the one before. All pain aside, death forces change and usually comes when it is most necessary for soul development.

I had an incident where crows were hunting me…They were literally following me everywhere and dive-bombing me when I would go to my car. They had taken up residence in the trees outside my house and were there pretty much all day. They weren't attacking me, in the strictest sense of the word, but they definitely wanted to let me know that they were around and they were unhappy with me. I started hating them. To the best of my ability I tried to make peace with them for my past transgressions…(I had inadvertently been stealing their food) but they still followed me around for weeks. What I didn't understand until it was pointed out

The Soul System of Tarot

to me – the crows wanted to help me change psychologically. They wanted to teach me to think differently and were actually doing me a favor with their presence.

You see I had been going through a very difficult spiritual time. I was having problems making progress and letting go of old patterns. Unbeknownst to myself, I was in need of some external guidance. This had been a very painful lesson: the crows were on the verge of driving me mad, I mean Edgar Alan Poe style mad! All manner of uncomfortable thoughts were running through my head at that time. I guess you can say that I had faced my own death. It forced me to bravely move ahead in my life, even though I had convinced myself that they were actively trying to kill me.

Most people wouldn't have said that death was looming over me, but in fact it was a psychological death. The crows were pointing out errors in my thinking process. These errors were driving me further away from myself and into the arms of the psychotic world. I will always remember the crows' generosity – their attempt to help me overcome my emotional and spiritual developmental battles. Part of me had lost hope. They helped me to regain that hope, albeit in a very unconventional and confrontational way. I now understand that the omens and lessons of all of nature's creations must be followed. The crows, in particular, represent the Plutonic guardians of this realm. They represent the lines of reality we are not allowed to cross. If we veer outside of the purview of our human behavioral boundaries they will be there promptly to let us know. Every realm has rules to one degree or another and I think the crows represent a gatekeeper caste in a way.

Chapter 1

The Daily Draw Practice

Practice...Because Practice Makes Perfect!

For years I have drawn three cards in the morning and asked those three cards to show me a focus, or direction to follow for the day. I think this ritual has been very beneficial: it has allowed me to learn the card's definitions at my own comfortable pace. It also allowed me to observe predictive energy cycles in a low-pressure environment. Which in effect, served to reinforce my intuitive understandings of my life's more subtle predicative energy patterns. Most importantly, this process will allow you to trust yourself and the spiritual choices you make.

What do I mean by this? There have been umpteen times that I have been offered a job. Then I run the cards and realize that the person offering the job was of low moral standing and would effectively drain my spiritual energy. I'm not saying I have never taken one of these jobs, it really depends on the reading's individualistic message. Sometimes other cards reinforce the fact that although there are emotional or personal difficulties with the gig, there will be other transformative experiences to be had as well. Even when forced to work with evil or problematic people, good things can emerge. I personally reject the idea that life is meant to be experienced only in a safety sealed environment. The Tao Te Ching states: what is a good man but a bad man's teacher? Sometimes it doesn't matter what color the cat is as long as he catches the rat. My most notable experience in this regard was when I ran my moving company. I had a partner who was an ex-convict. He was a really nice dude and was extremely appreciative just to be living a normal life and have a good gig. The guy actually went on to run the company by himself after I left. Moral of the story being, you just never know what growth lies in the unexpected facets of life.

I'm also not saying that you should base your entire life on the cards or readings, as this can be another common trap people fall into when they first start to dive into the work. I have seen many beginning practitioner's fall into a codependent obsessive pattern of doing readings in an effort to micromanage their future. Essentially this pattern digresses into doing readings to see if they should take out the trash or take a walk. (I know this sounds ridiculous but it's more common than you think). I fell into this trap myself. I was enduring one of life's rough patches. I was desperately wishing that the cards would offer hope. Sadly, the cards aren't designed for being your codependent crutch. They can provide some hope, but at that point you have to act upon the advice in order to receive benefit. The hope from the cards is a temporary fix. It doesn't last long. On the other hand being a righteous person and performing righteous deeds along your life journey produces a sustainable form of happiness, so I would say it's preferable overall.

This neurotic card reading I have dubbed "predictive addiction". It's a sort of anxiety about making any small error in your decision making process. Trying to micro manage your fate isn't possible, nor is it healthy. The Dao advises people to always go with the flow…I fully support this advice because under most circumstances

The Soul System of Tarot

overthinking will stress you out and cut you off from your intuitive voice. Tarot should be implemented with a "set it and forget it type mentality". You use it, consider it and then walk away, enough said.

If you do find yourself acting neurotically, put the cards down and think about it for a second. Will knowing the future really spare you from having to confront your destiny? Try to step back and realize that the Tarot is a tool: it is not to be abused like some drug. If you have to, limit yourself to one reading a day. Or set limits as to what life situations deserve a reading. You also need to be able to how to embrace life's spontaneous and mysterious dimensions, so sometimes its better not to know!

Heed the Warnings of the Tarot!

So lets say you have developed a healthy relationship with your readings and are asking legitimate long-term questions that require qualified third party guidance. Then you ask a question that comes back with a few "warning" type cards. You should take a moment and really analyze how these feelings hit you internally? Does the information resonate with you on a deep level, or do you feel as though the warnings are unwarranted? There have definitely been times when I didn't follow the warning/guidance of the cards and have lost sums of money, become sick, or wasted days of my life on fruitless pursuits. Time and energy which might have been saved had I heeded the warning provided to me by my little mystical amigos.

Here is when it becomes tricky and unpredictable: sometimes the cards will point you in a direction that is 180 degrees from where you thought that your day was headed (this is where self-trust becomes key). This can come in the form of a warning of emotional distress, economic upheaval or a delay or suspension of existing plans. Many times this can leave you uncertain and sometimes feeling a bit hopeless. There have been times when I had a "big day" planned with many different activities and events on the docket, only to learn that the cards said everything I had been working towards was going to go up in flames. How about this for a difficult reading: you meet a prospective mate (guy or gal). You are energized. This person has relationship potential. Then the cards reveal that this soul mate is an unbalanced, lying, cheating, psychologically disturbed, hedonistic, spiritually devoid, nut-job…trust me, if you're single and do readings long enough, this will happen to you at least once.

The really sobering part about practicing the Tarot is that you will begin to realize just how screwed up most people really are. When practicing the Tarot with pure intent and a correct deck, you can make great strides in developing psychological insights into the world around you. The cards truly don't lie, as the cheeseball fake TV psychic "Ms. Cleo" has touted in the past. They will point you towards the truth, even when that truth is the last thing you want to hear. Many people hate the truth. Many people can't handle the truth and heck, many people flat out run from the truth. Again, I emphasize, the root word for Tarot, comes from the root word "truth." The cards will teach you how to accept reality on its own terms – you will develop a rock solid intuitive discernment which will protect you from people, places, events, or energies which would serve to throw you off of your spiritual "A" game!

What makes a chess master a chess master? It's because that master is seventeen steps ahead of any move his opponent might

The Soul System of Tarot

make. Before the match has even begun, the master has actually defeated his opponent in his or her mind. Before the competition even starts the master has already assessed his opponent's movements, knows his opponent's style, understands his opponent's tired little diversions and is prepared to wait patiently until he can lure his opponent into checkmate. This is exactly how reality operates on the higher levels: there are untold pawns, rooks, and other characters put in place, which force us to use our higher spiritual abilities. If it weren't for a powerful foe, how would we ever discover the depths of our strength? While most others are shivering under the covers you can be out there on the battlefield developing a life for the history books. Fear is the only thing holding you back, so pick up the swords of the Tarot and get to work!

Chapter 2

The Calculations

Daily and Monthly Card Calculations!

The Universal Energy Cards of the day will show you what baseline energies the cosmos offer us on any particular day.

Your internal feelings/environment card

This card will reveal your internal temperament and what kind of thought process you can expect to experience on this day. No matter if it's a very cerebral day or just a good day for staying close to home and studying, there is always a way to utilize the energies presented to us in any given day. Within nature nothing ever goes to waste. If there is one thing that God or the Tao or nature is, it is utilitarian. Even if the day predicts an emotionally unsettling energy, at bare minimum you will be able to understand and plan accordingly. This will prevent you from becoming frazzled when supposedly "unexpected" challenges emerge. You will be given the opportunity to let go of any attachment to the challenge by seeing it in its proper light. You will begin to understand how the challenges of the day are really just a part of a larger, societally based energy cycle and not necessarily something happening to you alone.

How To Calculate the Internal Personal Day Card

So say you want to understand what the overall universal energies are going to be around you on any particular day, you can do that quite easily! First off add the numerical month number: aka January=1, February=2, and so on up to 12. Then add that to the day. November 5th would be 11+5=16. Then take the number and look up the corresponding card in table 1.4.

Now you might be asking: the table only goes up to 40, what if the dates add up to a number larger than that? Say with December 29th. Once past 40 it starts back to 1 again. So 41=1, 42=2, 43=3 and so on. (This is because every cycle repeats itself in time.) Again this card reveals how you will be feeling about yourself on any particular day. It also reveals the thoughts going through others' minds. Being that everyone is psychologically linked allows us to understand how this isn't a mystery. Since we are all on earth together, why would we not have to undergo the same energetic psychological forces? It only makes sense that our species would have to undergo similar spiritual "waves" of energy. As Jim Rohn once said: "The same wind blows upon us all." If this weren't the case then astrology would not pan out as a verifiable predictive phenomenon either. However you look at it, if you start analyzing these cyclical phenomenon for yourself, then you will start to understand their deeper significance within our lives.

Now you may be saying, wait if these cycles do add up to be static with regards to the internal card (i.e. January first will always add up to being a 2 of wands internal card no matter what year it is) then how come every year isn't exactly the same? This is a valid question. Yes, every year may have some of the same internal

THE SOUL SYSTEM OF TAROT

building blocks, but how we translate that into our greater reality is what really makes up the energies of that particular day. Look at July the 4th for example. It is a day for celebrating the Declaration of Independence in America. Even though, historically speaking, this wasn't the official date when everyone was able to sign it, it is a date ruled by the ace of cups. The ace of cups is a very creative and emotional card: it inspires hope and renewal so it becomes the perfect day for this kind of holiday to take place. Or take Valentines Day for Example, this is an energy of the 6 of Cups which specifically rules dating. Or on the darker side it can represent lust and false love. In my humble opinion, there are no accidents and the reasons these dates have been chosen is not accidental either. People in ages past used these types of modalities to plan these things out. Of course I don't know which ones exactly, but I can assure you that holidays which are not in harmony with these energies will not last long. Christmas is an interesting one because the 7 of pentacles represent it. In essence it is supposed to represent the opposite of commercialism and the need for a sense of patience and true purpose in life. This holiday has obviously been perverted over the years, but it's interesting to note that these probably were the puritanical ideals in which the holiday was first conceived. Again, for more in depth card definitions/discussions please see Mr. Tsarion's pioneering root work, *The Path of the Fool*.

What to look for from your External circumstances/environment card

This card governs how those around you will behave and the energetic influences that you will encounter at this time. This can show you whether you should be focusing more energy internally or externally, depending upon the day's personal goals. Some days our opportunities are internal. Some days they will be external. The point is: these cards will show us what to look for. It will also show you the energetic playing field of that day's particular situations or circumstances whatever they may be. Some of the darker cards might present us with more problematic situations or people but we must take this in stride. Just because we have an 8 of swords or other, more unsavory card, it doesn't mean you need to hide under the covers. But it does mean that you should be more cognizant of your surroundings. Heed any subtle warnings your subconscious provides and realize that where there is smoke there is usually fire!

How to Calculate the External Personal Day Card

So basically all you do for the external card is add the sum total of the year to the personal day card total. So lets say the personal day card was 17. You would add the numerical year total 2+0+1+5=8 to the personal day card which is 17. So 17+8 is 25! Simple right? Then all you need do is to look it up in the same table.

How to Calculate Your Personal Month Cards...

So these cards are a bit different as they can correlate to both the major and minor arcana. I like to look up both. This is another simple calculation – just add the month number with the year number. Let's take August 2015. August=8 plus 2015=8 so we end up with 8+8=16. This will correlate with both the Tower (the 16th card in the major arcana) and the 6 of cups. Now you can begin to understand the overarching lessons and playing field for the month.

The Soul System of Tarot

This branches off to an understanding of the deeper patterns. By studying those around you, you can see who is learning and progressing through these cycles in a spiritual way and who is choosing to ignore the lessons that these cycles represent. By observing these cycles long enough you will develop a profound understanding about life itself. I will present more cases studies of this in subsequent works and on my website: www.astrologybyaustin.com.

Things to think about when utilizing the personal energetic cards!

Depending on a person's personal chart/cards there can be umpteen ways this energy is externally expressed. Yet running your daily cards will allow an understanding of your underlying motivations for that particular day/time. It will also describe the types of circumstances you will encounter for that date. Another way to look at the energy would be to identify it as the daily collective lesson for humanity. If you are experiencing a card's negative attributes you are not acting in accordance with your higher spiritual motivations. Generally speaking, if you are not following your internal higher spiritual compass you will face more difficulties. Common sense, right? If you are able to squeeze a couple of good deeds into your day you will be much better off. You can avoid the dangers of the more negative cards by exhibiting a pure evolutionary intent within your day-to-day actions. Life always offers temptations and evil choices – it's up to us to resist them.

Another helpful tool is waking up in the morning and immediately rising. It's important to honor these cosmic wakeup calls, so that you are able to utilize all of your day's personal energy to the fullest. The caveat here being that if you are having energy problems or health issues, you may need some healing before these cosmic wake up calls come into full effect. Going back to sleep can produce bad dreams and you will awaken feeling much worse than when you woke up initially. I know it can be difficult to wake up and pop out of bed, but once you get the hang of it, it's not so difficult. Sleeping too much is a sign of depression and I feel it exhibits a lack of faith in your spiritual quest here on earth. If we cannot maximize the finite spiritual energies to produce something, then how can we expect to be given more energy when we are sleeping away the energy that we have already been given?

Let me clarify this – I have encountered much personal suffering during my life. I understand just how difficult it is to live a fully exerted spiritually motivated existence. Heck some days its hard just getting out of bed, let alone trying to master the complexities of your own internal universe. I still feel that when we make sincere attempts at personal reformation, the universe will always support us in these endeavors, no matter how small our efforts may seem at the time.

Having cognition of the days more prone to difficulty, you can work on actively transcending the day's circumstantial dark energy. Many times, we have a tendency to become our own worst enemy. The daily indicator cards can present warnings that can keep you from doing anything self-destructive on days prone to such activities. There is a phrase in Daoism, which seems simple but is inherently profound, "take the good and leave the bad". If we are able to leave behind our lower self-destructive patterns, the universe can then find higher-level spiritual tasks for us to pursue.

The Soul System of Tarot

Take myself for example: I started out at the bottom of the bottom when it comes to a career/vocational track (fast food and manual labor to be specific). I also suffered from an entitlement mentality and I had a chip on my shoulder. I thought someone of my skill set should be occupying a higher-level position of some sort. Poverty and grunt work is life's way of beating the ego out of you with poverty and grunt work. There is no room for ego when you are at the bottom of the totem pole. I guess you could say that I suffered from the all too common "millennial" poor work ethic. But after much self-reformation and having had worked at over 30 different jobs I was able to transcend my narrow viewpoint. Even though I still undergo the daily struggle for metaphysical freedom, at least I am involved in a more meaningful kind of work. I feel like everyday I wake up contributes to something greater within the larger sphere of the human experience. I know that my effort works to bring harmony to those around me. This fills me with a deep sense of satisfaction that inspires me to keep moving forward.

I was also able to give up some bad habits, cultivate some discipline, and free myself from the conventional work matrix. I don't believe that anyone should be under the illusion that working at your dream life is going to be an easy process. I highly doubt anything in this life is that easy, but that's just me. I personally had to dig for many years to pull my vocational dreams out of myself. They had been buried under misinterpreted memories of misfortune, so I had to dig them out. I'm praying that you have an easier go at life than I have had. All I know is that eventually hard work and self-discipline becomes the key to pretty much all of life. The good news is that when it comes to hard work and self-discipline, nobody can take your efforts away from you. They might be able to take away your riches or your intellectual accolades, but the internal strength you gain during this life is yours to keep.

Many times in life it's hard to truly appreciate how far we have come. It's hard to understand the visceral forms of suffering as we experienced them in the moment. Although I can assure you that no matter what you think once you reach your vocational destination, the struggle is real. The pain of this life is also real, albeit temporal. The good news is that, that same pain will in time become your strength. Trees subjected to the strongest winds, produces the strongest roots. So never fear your struggles, for they are forcing you to continually strengthen your roots and grow fuller leaves.

To some degree, I guess you could say that we suffer on this plane only as long as we choose to. When we whole-heartedly decide to leave the chaotic patterns of this world behind, we can also leave behind the sorrows and the karmic hardships as well. When you are on a life track dedicated towards continual self-improvement a higher work ethic must be maintained, but there are also less hellish psychological battles to fight in order to stay on track. The cool thing about getting stronger spiritually is that you are able to accomplish much more than others who lack clarity of thought, while maintaining a greater sense of internal peace.

To recap: when you're looking at these cards/definitions keep in mind the fact that you can personally transcend the energy of any universal day. This may require what seems to be an extraordinary amount of effort, but I am here to tell you that it's definitely possible. On the days containing the most overt dark energy, (for lack of a better term) I have still been able to transcend the day's circumstances and bring value to my own life and that of my clientele. Utilizing this daily card guide in conjunction with a few

The Soul System of Tarot

other calendars and apps that I recommend will give you a firm foundation for successful day-to-day planning.

Other Planning/Astrology systems I recommend include...

- Timegnosis.com

- The Moon Deluxe App (IPhone and Android)

- Chinese Horoscopes by Buzly Labs

By utilizing these invaluable planning tools in conjunction with your daily Tarot card analysis, it will give you full spectrum breakdown of that day's unique energy! Understanding what life will be bringing forth makes life easier, because with understanding comes mental preparedness and acceptance. When we accept this world for what it is and understand the human failings within others and ourselves we can then begin to transcend the energy by transmuting it.

How to Calculate your Personal Year Result Card

This card will represent a major theme for your year. What your overarching lesson is and what you need to focus on in order to be really successful.

First off you need to lookup your Life Path Year Card, which is governed by your birth year. You will then subtract the current year card i.e. 2016=9 (The Hermit) from the number associated with your total year card, i.e. The fool=0 The magician=1 The high priestess=2 and so on...) Once you subtract one from the higher numbered card from the lower numbered card, then you will have the theme card for your own personal year. So for example, if your Life Path Card was "The Lovers" which equals 6, you would take that and subtract it from the yearly card "The Hermit" which equals 9. This would give you 3 so it would mean that your final result would be "The Empress".

So for you, this might be a more laid back year, focusing on a need for self-motivation. It may be easier to focus on love and relationships, but the need for creativity should not be neglected!

How to Calculate your Tarot/Saturn Cycles

Life Phase #1 (1st Saturn revolution)

0-30 years old

Externalized Self Governed by your Major Arcana card in the personal spread. This corresponds with your card number in Table 1.1.

So, from 0-30 years old: you are actually in your first cycle of time, which corresponds, to your Saturn return. The first thirty-year cycle mostly deals with coming to terms with your externalized ego self. Being that Saturn is the master teacher in the zodiac and perhaps one of the overlords of cyclical time phases, it has a large influence in our lives when it moves around the entirety of our chart once every 30 years. In astrology the longer a cycle takes to complete, the more powerful and subtle it is overall. Even though it may have dramatic effects, many times we can't see it, because it happens gradually over such a long period of time. The thing is if you have a difficult arcana card here then you and those born in your personal year might be

THE SOUL SYSTEM OF TAROT

late bloomers unless you are able to somehow, expeditiously conquer the challenges associated with the card. If you have an easier card then your youth might very well be a happier time in your life. Either way there's pros and cons so just enjoy what you can, when you can because life happiness is never guaranteed. Normally we have to go out and create happiness for ourselves. When this cycle is completed we are ready to separate the wheat from the chaff. If you can really individuate and do your thing after 30, you can become a tour de force in society. At that point our vocational development can help you build good karma and make positive internal change for yourself. This is why you find people switching occupations around their Saturn return. That subconscious drive to find more meaning kicks in for some people and they are then able to pursue greater heights in that capacity of their life. The first 30 years are primarily about developing confidence in yourself and your capacities whatever they may be. After 30 you can start to focus a bit more on others. Unless you started having a family early, in which case your attentions can be diverted sooner than 30.

Life Phase #2 (2nd Saturn Revolution)

30-60 Years Old Worldly Accomplishments Cycle

This phase is where you face the world and accomplish things based upon a grander desire to shape society at large. This is accomplished in a million different ways. During this time, you should focus on aspects of your vocational self, located in position 2 on the Tarot spread. At this time you can work on answering the deeper purpose driven career life questions. (For this I would also advise consulting my prior book "Startup Fever" which may also aid in your question for vocational motivation.) If you are able to embody the positive traits of your vocational card then this should be a really positive and straight ahead time. But if you step meekly toward your goals or you are unable to find meaningful work within the context of your archetypal nature then you may be in for a bumpier ride. It all comes down to personal effort, a dedication to spiritual progression and a willingness to give up our old ways of being. If that can be accomplished, then all doors will start to open all on their own.

It may be hard to tangibly understand, but when we start to change, then the universe starts to change as a result of our progression. Hence when a tree grows tall and strong it provides a shelter from the storm which was previously unavailable. So in essence, our personal changes can draw others towards us, or push others away. Either way it has some effect. This is why a dedication to personal development is so important. People want to be around inspirational people, not hang out with the town drunk. It seems common sense but putting it into this framework shows us how important it is for us to go out and make our dreams come true, because our efforts will eventually inspire others around us to do their best as well. This is the way the whole world can get better in time, despite how terrible things may seem at the moment.

Life Phase 3 (3rd Saturn Revolution)

60-90 Self-acceptance and internal struggle

During this life phase you have hopefully learned to accept yourself for yourself. You can now begin to transcend your unique personality archetype in order to help others to truly understand themselves and their deeper meanings in the cosmos. Obviously the best thing to do during a phase like this would be to teach those that will listen about what you have learned and to continue internal personal development. It's a time for internal development and (if finances allow) pursuing personal passions that you may not have had time to pursue in other life phases! This corresponds with the court royals card, which is card number 3 in your personal Tarot spread!

Life Phase #4 (4th Saturn Revolution)

No cards are associated with this phase!

This is a phase where we have effectively transcended our archetypes and are able to pursue our lives free from the typical societal constraints, given that we have stored up enough vitality to keep going strong at this age. Life will become ever more meaningful by the day and death or immortality starts to creep into consciousness. If you have been a saintly figure you may be able to ascend to higher realms during this time, or if you have made mistakes in the past you should work on taking care of any kind of unfinished business or unsettled relationships before you leave earth. The less unfinished business you have on your plate, the more likely it is that you will be able to expedite your spiritual journey to whatever destination the universe has for you. Taoists try to live as long as possible because they believe that no matter what happens, if you don't live long enough you won't really have time to truly understand the nature of reality itself.

Chapter 3

Why bother with a spiritual/divination practice?

Taoist theory says that no energy in the universe is ever wasted. In the highest forms of spiritual development, the practitioner maintains a path that emphasizes continual advancement. Again, this advanced spiritual lifestyle is quite difficult as the universe's counterpointing evil force is as powerful as hell (literally speaking). Yet dimensions of existence only have as much power over us as we give them. Dimensions are constructed with the same spiritual energies used to create the universe, it's just that some dimensions are tuned to another frequency so to speak. Without the spiritual energy present, hell would not get very far. Heaven can exist without hell, but hell cannot exist without heaven as evil eventually consumes itself. As Lao Tsu states in the Tao Te Ching, "anything that is not Tao-like, soon ceases to exist."

Heaven on the other hand is eternally regenerative and inexhaustible. Obviously reality's darker dimensions also have a purpose or they would not exist. Since we live in a very utilitarian universe, rest assured that everything, no matter how small, serves some purpose. If a dimension is "real" so to speak, then there's a need to exercise reverence that will take care of the dimension and prevent it from becoming transformed into something really dark. Focusing on our own inner psychic purification is what starts this process.

When we begin to transmute these seemingly negative energies in our own body, we can then begin to see our deeper soul purpose through all of the events in our daily life. When you're truly living on your personal highest path everything becomes that much more meaningful. This fact is what people need to realize when utilizing this text. Every life event attempts to teach us how to maintain internal balance while dealing with the up-and-down energetic fluctuations of daily life. Life is the greatest teacher any of us will ever encounter. Life works to break us down on all levels, leaving only our base spiritual essence at the end of the process. Life in essence becomes a form of spiritual alchemy. The Tarot is our companion along this alchemical journey – it enlightens us as to the traditional speed bumps faced during the fool's journey back to selfhood.

The Tarot speaks to us on an archetypal symbolic level. This is why it is so effective. Bypassing the ego's drama helps the cards get to the root of the issue every time. It works to demystify the trials that we all face at one point or another if we live long enough. Trials such as birth, reaching maturity, dealing with power structures in the world, receiving wisdom from worldly teachers, experiencing the death of a loved one, finding a meaningful profession, transcending materialism, getting married, raising children, becoming a mentor and so on. These archetypal events are laid out for us in the Tarot through the concept of the Fools Journey of the Major Arcana. The fool starts out as a babe and ends up as a spiritually transcendent being at the end of his journey through the Major Arcana.

THE SOUL SYSTEM OF TAROT

If we can take these inherent life trials and work with them, then we will be able to successfully master the experience of being a successful and spiritually integrated human being – a task that I believe we were all sent here to accomplish in one form or another. Yet if we fail to learn these lessons and instead choose to stick our head in the sand, then there is a price to pay. Life wasn't given to us so we can waste it, it was given to you so that you could go into the world and create purpose. Only a fool thinks that he will be able to master the entirety of the physical world. The world answers to no one. The Tao answers to no one, but according to the Tao Te Ching and Lao Tzu heaven will always help the good man or woman.

So when you look up these definitions for your day-to-day insight and usage, look at them neither pessimistically nor optimistically. Instead try and feel out the middle point between the two because as Murphy's Law states, things can still go wrong at any time. Any type of despotic, egotistical or narcissistic manipulation of others will always hurt your chances at sustainable success. I believe that there is no point in life when we should be over-confident. Evil will always exist on this plane of existence and nothing we can do will change that. This dimension was set up that way for a purpose. It is our job to understand the purpose of evil. I believe that death actually protects life, because without death, evil would perpetuate itself forever instead of being forced into other dimensions. So in that respect, death definitely deserves our sincere appreciation.

A spiritual person cannot underestimate the internal and external perils ever present on earth. Evil is devious because it is an expert at disguising itself. It can manifest externally in the form of a real world struggle, or it can goad us towards self-sabotage from within.

Austin Muhs

It may sound exhausting being on guard around the clock against evil, but in my experience at the higher levels, this is what is required. Again this isn't a bad thing, the world is trying to help us by presenting us internal and external evils that must be conquered in order to strengthen our spiritual defenses. I believe there has to be more enlightened life forms beyond this earth and the enormous amount of personal and existential suffering that takes place here.

    Always remember that foreknowledge is power, but the Tarot will help you only to the degree that you are committed to helping yourself. A halfhearted attempt at personal development can be a dangerous game. Why? The answer is: there are no Archimedean points in life where the universe will stop giving you ever more difficult challenges to conquer. Evil will always want to bring you down and good things will always bring you up. Looking for a destination point within your spiritual studies or a way to halt your personal developmental efforts is like looking for a place to take a nap in the middle of the river: even if you are perched on a solid raft, there is no guarantee that you won't end up encountering a waterfall downstream. The strange truth of our reality is its perpetual nature, obviously death will meet us at one point or another, but for those wholeheartedly committed to spiritual progression, that journey never stops! For as the saying goes, if you're not living then you're dying…

    Is spiritual development supposed to stop when you get that perfect life for yourself? What will happen when you finally get the car, the spouse, the house and the peace of mind? Will the spiritual trials suddenly disappear? I don't believe so. In fact, major external achievements might just serve to exacerbate the spiritual trials that you face. Always be prepared for the long haul and be prepared for

The Soul System of Tarot

anything. No one knows what life may bring, but if you prepare a solid internal foundation then you will have a good chance for cumulative Dharmic attainment.

Chapter 4

Procedural Advice On Doing Readings...

Looking up your day ahead in this book might just represent a good first step in crafting a meaningful morning ritual. Before the reading I always light some incense in honor of the higher spiritual beings in the universe and I recite the following prayer for clarity! (Feel free to modify it as you see fit...)

"Please let this reading be for my highest spiritual good. I pray and give thanks to all the benevolent spiritual beings who have come before me and who aid me in this reading. Please show me what I should I focus on for the day." Or "Please show (clients name) potential successes and/or pitfalls next 3-6 months" or whatever length of time you are trying to do a reading for. Yet I find Tarot is most helpful when looking for a year or less ahead into the future!

Then I proceed to shuffle and draw the cards. Again, when looking at the cards, you are trying to visualize your days/weeks/months events that have been plotted out so far and how these cards may tell a story relating to these events. Without this kind of forward thinking analysis you might end up being a bit perplexed at your answers. There are also instances where the cards will either warn you or try to convince you to focus on a totally different subject. Perhaps you have been consumed by work and the cards want you to focus on your spiritual pursuits instead. If this is the case you may see the 10 of pentacles come up. Or you may get the 10 of wands to show that you have been over exerting yourself, trying to carry the world on your shoulders. Alternatively, you may draw the 4 of swords; this means that it's time to take a time out and contemplate other actions. The four of swords in particular warns against burning the candle at both ends or your health will suffer as a result. If you are supposed to continue in the same direction, you might get the 8 of pentacles, 2 of wands, 8 of wands, 3 of pentacles just to name a few. You need to learn the definitions of these cards like the back of your hand. They all have very individualistic nuances that you may not understand unless you know the cards front to back.

Why Less, Really is More!

I guess you could say that I am a bit more informal than others in my field and perhaps you would be right, but then again I don't wear a cape nor do I don a turban during my readings either. I always try to opt for the most simplistic approach. Here is why.

Say I am stranded in the desert with a broken down car. All I have is my deck and a glass of water. If I need to see which direction to go for repairs or assistance, am I going to lose faith in the cards due to my lack of accessories (i.e. crystal ball, incense, turban, cape)? No, I will promptly do my reading, follow my intuition and proceed to get the heck out of the desert. In my opinion there is no silly pomp and circumstance needed for the cards to work. All of that other stuff is merely for showmanship and perhaps to mask a lack of real skill.

I do believe you should dress semi-professionally just so people who place a high value upon appearances take you seriously. But

The Soul System of Tarot

fashion sense shouldn't come into play when dealing with your client's problem. The more pomp and circumstance I see in life, the more suspicious I become. If someone is trying too hard to impress you with their flashy nature, usually it is because they are hiding a deep-seated insecurity of some kind. These are the reasons why I try to keep my style minimalist. I want my words to be the focus of my reading, not magic crystals or some old song and dance routine.

Where to do a reading!

There are many different places one could do a reading: in a bedroom, in a café, in a park, in an office etc. Pragmatically speaking wherever you end up doing the reading, you should always adjust and go with the flow of your environment. If you were stranded at a circus, perhaps a cape and face paint would be a good call, but when you are doing simple readings for yourself or for someone at a coffee shop, then try and match the professional attire of those who frequent the establishment. You blend in and will be able to do your readings in peace. The Tarot naturally attracts attention. Most of the attention is a distraction and semi-problematic so the more low-key you can make your readings the better. Telling the future makes some people insecure – they don't want to believe such a thing is possible. So you mitigate that with kindness and being upfront about your readings and intentions. And, never, ever, try to solicit another client while doing a reading even if they are asking for your info. It's in poor form and the inquirer's behavior borders on rudeness. It's an invasion of privacy and makes your client feel strange.

Honestly, my favorite place to do readings is outside in nature. Café's can have a questionable energetic disposition and doing it at your house isn't usually the best idea either. Brining someone's energy into your home is a very questionable practice, because you don't know what you're letting through the door. Just like any psychologist when you are treating a client you will start to bring out that person's insecurities and neurotic tendencies, so you have to be on guard. This means keeping them out of the house. From time to time some people will become reactionary or go into denial mode. Others will become really sad so you need to be sensitive with how you deliver the information.

Every person is different. Some people can handle more information than others. Your job as the reader is to take note of this and understand which clients are capable of handling what information. Putting them on spiritual reformation overload won't work unless they are already highly committed to their own personal development. Encourage them with baby steps. Have them come back every 3-6 months for a progress checkup where they will learn of additional areas where they might be able to improve.

The cool thing about this is that your skill set as a reader will always be improving. If you are serious about personal skill studies then you will always learn something new that you can apply to your client. Your new abilities will allow you to see client's problem with an intuitive, clearer vision. Spiritual truth is a relative phenomenon based upon our current, always changing level of awareness. The truth we impart upon others should always be changing as well. The bottom line is you have to trust yourself. Always remember, you are on a long road towards personal enrichment.

Inevitably you will end up with clients who want to pursue a more personal relationship. This is never to be pursued. It represents codependent energy right from the relationship's start. Plus you can't really expect your clients to be 100 percent honest since they are coming to you for spiritual guidance.

Remember, clients will sometimes present you with a problem that you yourself might be facing on some internal level. The better job you do helping your clients heal themselves, the better that you in turn will be healed. Working for others is really working for yourself as well, as long as that person isn't actively trying to abuse you somehow. In the Tao Te Ching, Lao Tzu states "What is a good man, but a bad mans teacher?" Simple words, but infinitely profound when taken in context with this type of healing work.

Long story short, locations are important as they can be empowering to people. Getting a reading in a place that possesses bad Feng Shui can add another degree of mental pressure to your client's already apprehensive mindset.

But when you conduct your readings in a place that is in harmony with nature then everyone is at ease and more willing to assimilate the information, good or bad, learned from the reading.

Chapter 5

How to Construct Your Personal Tarot Chart

To varying degrees, your Major Arcana Archetype card (the one found on Table 1.1) will govern the first 30 years of you. The cards represent your karmic influences from past lives. Those born during more difficult yearly phases will generally face more challenges than those born in easier going years…If we analyze this trend in the long-term, we will begin to understand that this chain of destined events is systemic. What do I mean by this? For example, suppose you are born in a year governed by a difficult Tarot card (i.e. Tarot. Chariot. Hanged man). You will then be subconsciously linked with others in your peer group who share the same year. Obviously you will face many of the same challenges as others in your exact age range. I believe that this is divine intervention, so humans can help one another with similar problems.

Thinking back, most of my friends suffered through similarly dysfunctional family patterns, which served to hamper their long-term emotional and spiritual developmental cycles. Yet we somehow came to understand and empathize with one another's struggles and triumphs. I believe this is a divine blessing because without others around us suffering from similar karmic patterns we would feel even more alone and alienated in our suffering. I think that it is further testimony that we are never truly alone in the universe.

I think this is currently best exhibited by how the older generation treats the young. For the most part, the younger generation is getting a bad rap for being lazy, entitled brats within the corporate world. Not taking into account the fact that these are the same people that have largely allowed the media to raise their children for them, all the while wondering how their kids got all neurotic along the way. This, I feel, has to do with their archetypal cyclical viewpoint, as they have watched the familial dysfunction this corporate system breeds when put into effect long-term. So in essence they are subconsciously rebelling into a system that they feel is broken, sadly many of them rebel in an unhealthy and ineffectual manner. Whatever side of the argument you are on is really irrelevant, as you can still see how certain generational segments can be cast into a particular light. Using this as an example, you can easily see how this might hurt a younger person's long-term financial potential within the corporate structure. The lesson for the young clearly becomes a pattern where one works to transcend the current corporate paradigm (not a particularly simple task). But rest assured, in time, the problems of the previous era will be fixed. This will foster personal growth while allowing more spiritually enriching vocational cycles to come into being.

Now if you were born just 5-10 years earlier, (aka Generation X) then you might have gained an economic foothold on life during the dot com boom. Again I am creating hypotheticals just to illustrate the point demonstrated by particular cycles of time and their respective consequences. However you slice it, I think it's obvious that being born during an economic boom wave might be

The Soul System of Tarot

more enjoyable than an economic bust cycle such as the great depression. Yet, I would imagine at the same time that the hard times would almost always produce a more spiritually mature populace. I also feel that despite a reputation of futility, collective action can from time to time be a powerful agent for mass healing, especially during the younger years of your life. When this happens in a society, others can act as mirrors so that we are able to adjust socially by tackling the mass psychological maladies of the age together through self-awareness. Granted, people always go about this in different ways and people move at different speeds, but if people could be aware of the need for healing in general that would at least let the train pull out of the station. I would imagine that letting go of the fear associated with abandoning modern civilized life is a big hurdle towards this happening anytime soon.

Even though this type of group healing has been historically rare, I have to imagine that it is quite possible to achieve. I guess one could say that periods such as the renaissance resembled what the beginnings of such a healing era might look like. You could also make a case for some of the golden dynasties that took place under China's more benevolent monarchs (i.e. the Yellow Emperor, etc.). Periods where the arts were thriving and the human spirit was less restless and distracted than we currently find ourselves. During these times in history there was a relative sense of calm and human purpose seemed to be a bit more in harmony with the overarching vision of the leaders in charge.

So long-term is one Tarot card archetype better than another? That's for you to decide, I'm sure we have all wished we were in someone else's shoes at one point or another during our lives. Yet I feel the important thing to remember is that on earth, everyone has problems and everyone has some form of inherent karma to work out. If we didn't have karma, or psychological deficiencies, we wouldn't have wasted our time landing on this rock.

The more you deal with these cycles within your own life or your clients, the more you realized how deep the traumas on earth really run. As the Buddhists state, life is suffering to one degree or another. I personally believe there has to be a suffering free domain somewhere, but we humans, in order to earn our stripes, must evolve to embrace the characteristics of those higher realms. Earth is like a kindergarten for souls, a place where you learn how to share, not hit your neighbors during lunch and steal his candy bar.

So when you are looking up the definitions of these cards in the *Path of the Fool* by Michael Tsarion, keep in mind that you have been given whatever tools you need to complete your soul's spiritual quest. It is your responsibility to cast away the cobwebs and dig out these tools so you complete your grand quest. No matter what your external quest may be, you may take comfort in the fact that your external card just dictates your external circumstances during early life. Later in life I believe that we fully grow into our other cards. We grow into the internal and secret desires cards so that we rely less on the external world for fulfillment and instead start looking inwardly to draw our passion for life.

Time and again we are able to become what we once thought impossible. I remember the first time I saw someone skilled playing the guitar. I was four years old and I saw this gentleman in his mid 30s performing all of these complex finger movements while singing. It seemed impossible and, I imagine, for some it truly is. But low and behold my mind wanted to do that so badly the heavens opened up a path for me to discover just such abilities

The Soul System of Tarot

within myself. So no matter what your external card might be, you must remember two things:

> Number one, just because you have an externally pleasing card that gives you an easy start in life, doesn't mean that things will always be easy, or that your internal psychological state will always be rosy. Those who have it too easy are in danger of peaking too early therefore feeling unfulfilled after the life's "peak" experiences. This is dangerous. Spiritual cultivation is meant to be perpetual. The longer we get drawn into these unhealthy thoughts that the best parts of our life are behind us, the more we will lose touch with our inner spiritual quest. This is why it's best to have your spiritual life firmly in place before you reach the pinnacle of your career or familial successes. This way you stay humble and retain a solid sense of who you really are.

> And number two, if you have been gifted with a more difficult external card, you should remember that those with more difficult paths are generally able to evolve quicker psychologically speaking, so the depths of their wisdom can be more profound and allow them to go through life in a more ethical and self reliant fashion, both of which are cornerstones of true spiritual development. Take time to remind yourself how far you have come and how your failures have paid off the karmas of your past. Future victories are assured, as long as dedicated spiritual pursuits are maintained while embodying a serene sense of reverence and patience.

Austin Muhs

How to Determine Your Birth Year Card!

Here is the table for the card governing your birth year. In general, this card will dictate the first 30 years of your life and will give you much to think about during that span of time. How to navigate the external world and what your internal sense of life truly means to you. All of these questions will be answered through understanding the deeper meaning behind this card! Now this is a general cheat sheet based upon the cycles of time I have observed and the hundreds of different client case studies I have gone over with a fine-toothed comb.

So after you lookup your year, you should take some time to visit Michael Tsarion's book, entitled *The Path of the Fool* to re-read the definitions for your corresponding birth year card. Mr. Tsarion gives exhaustive definitions, which I won't do the injustice of rehashing when they have been so succinctly put forth in his seminal reference work. So go ahead and snag the E-book so you have a good way to navigate through all of this material. If you're on a serious budget, Biddy Tarot has definitions online as well, but they are just not nearly as accurate as Mr. Tsarion's that I have personally verified through my years of working with them.

You should then look at the attributes associated with the card, good and bad. How have these types of archetypes played a role in your life thus far? Have you been avoiding the main lessons of your card? Or have you mastered the baseline energies and are not yet ready to move into a higher sphere of your development? Perhaps you are under 30 and still struggling to embody these lessons and maximize your younger phase of life.

The Soul System of Tarot

This yearly card will determine how your life will flow up until your Saturn return is completed, right around 30 years old. It also represents how people view you externally with regards to your personal struggles within life. Not to say that the cycles totally go away at that point, but the effects of the card are lessened at that

Birth Year	Major Arcana	Birth Year	Major Arcana	Birth Year	Major Arcana	Birth Year	Major Arcana
1940	The Hierophant	1952	The Star	1964	The Chariot	1976	The Sun
1941	The Lovers	1953	The Moon	1965	Strength	1977	Aeon/Judgment
1942	The Chariot	1954	The Sun	1966	The Hermit	1978	The World
1943	Strength	1955	Aeon/Judgment	1967	The Wheel of Fortune	1979	The Fool
1944	The Hermit	1956	The World	1968	Justice/Adjustment	1980	The Magician
1945	The Wheel of Fortune	1957	The Fool	1969	The Hanged Man		
1946	Justice/Adjustment	1958	The Magician	1970	Death		
1947	The Hanged Man	1959	The High Priestess	1971	Art/Temperance		
1948	Death	1960	The Empress	1972	The Devil		
1949	Art/Temperance	1961	The Emperor	1973	The Tower		
1950	The Devil	1962	The Hierophant	1974	The Star		
1951	The Tower	1963	The Lovers	1975	The Moon		

Birth Year	Major Arcana	Birth Year	Major Arcana	Birth Year	Major Arcana	Birth Year	Major Arcana
1981	The High Priestess	1993	Art/Temperance	2005	The Emperor	2017	The Tower
1982	The Empress	1994	The Devil	2006	The Hierophant	2018	The Star
1983	The Emperor	1995	The Tower	2007	The Lovers	2019	The Moon
1984	The Hierophant	1996	The Star	2008	The Chariot	2020	The Sun
1985	The Lovers	1997	The Moon	2009	Strength	2021	Aeon/Judgment
1986	The Chariot	1998	The Sun	2010	The Hermit	2022	The World
1987	Strength	1999	Aeon/Judgment	2011	The Wheel of Fortune		
1988	The Hermit	2000	The World	2012	Justice/Adjustment		
1989	The Wheel of Fortune	2001	The Fool	2013	The Hanged Man		
1990	Justice/Adjustment	2002	The Magician	2014	Death		
1991	The Hanged Man	2003	The High Priestess	2015	Art/Temperance		
1992	Death	2004	The Empress	2016	The Devil		

Table 1.1

The Soul System of Tarot

point, so that you are free to start developing the more finite points of your spiritual self. Some people will feel much more free to exhibit their true passions after 30 as these cards can act like an albatross if they are challenging.

I remember growing up all of my fellow classmates in my grade level seemed to overall be a very determined, yet troubled lot. I guess this could be said of all humanity, but I remember my friends really getting put through the gauntlet as compared to those of other graduating classes. These cards represent the lessons of your youth in many ways and if you are able to overcome them, then you will have built a solid foundation for yourself to bring into adulthood.

This first phase of your life will define the overall foundation of your life. It represents the paramount challenge of the first 30 years of your life. If you refuse to conquer, or are unable to conquer the base lessons associated with your first phase major arcana card, then you will be forced to proceed into your life with a shaky foundation. Although habits can always be changed, good habits are most easily formed early in life.

Depending on the astrological consistency of your personal natal chart, change may come easily, or it may be quite difficult for you to accept. I can say for a fact that whatever trials you are given in life, it is 100 percent possible to supersede them with enough spiritual effort. It is in no way my intention to tinge this book with a dogmatic perspective of life, quite the inverse. I want to give you the tools that allow you to give one hundred and twenty percent of your efforts towards crafting your own unique destiny.

On the other hand, I do want to be honest about revealing the full scope of any trials that you will face in life. Some people have modest hills to overcome during their lives, while other's trails are more akin to climbing Mount Everest. Perspective is relative, I guess. People born in the USA must have good fortune – unless you were born in the extreme hood, physical violence is probably lower here than in many other countries, not to mention that economic advancement is more difficult in other countries as well. Wherever you stand on the karmic difficulty scale you should realize that you wouldn't have chosen this life if you thought you couldn't handle it. While some of us might have bitten off more than we can chew, spiritual challenges wouldn't be profitable for our souls if they were not inherently difficult. That's why they are called challenges for Pete's sake.

As a small child, I felt as though I was always able to put my suffering into perspective. I didn't attach to it. I just rolled with the punches. I didn't understand that my family life was abnormally chaotic. Nor did I understand the fact that people took all of these adult concepts so seriously. I was just living the experience and letting life throw me around as it saw fit. This is the beauty of childhood: it's the freedom of innocence and openness to all experience that eventually molds us into a finite self. What a beautiful process don't you think?

It wasn't until I was in my teens that I really started to internalize my suffering and view myself as a victim of fate. You know those golden years when you pin all of your personal happiness on the approval of everyone else in your peer group? The cool thing about small kids is that they don't really need approval, they are going to do what they will. Children are able to better deal with difficulties because they don't naturally attach themselves to earthly suffering like teens and adults do. As a child your head is most definitely still in the clouds. Sadly enough, children do subconsciously absorb energy patterns from those around them, (namely from their parents) but beyond that they are able to naturally heal themselves as their internal balancing mechanisms are still in harmony with the heavens. It isn't until later in life where the school system, a lack of nature and other desecrated social cultures beat these systems into submission. At which point the children are left defenseless in a foreign land.

Perhaps if nobody ever told these kids how "difficult" his or her life has been, then they would not self ascribe all of the depression and personal angst to their past like I had done. Don't get me wrong, I am not trying to take away from the legitimate sufferings of human life, I am just searching for sustainable solutions to a world in emotional crisis. I feel like suffering is worse when we burn it into our brains that we have suffered or are victims. If someone never told you that you were broken, then would you still feel so damaged or like an outcast? I don't know, I just feel these are questions that should be answered.

In many ways I feel like our lives are only as tragic as we make them out to be. It all comes down to perspective. There are no innocent victims, as the karmic systems in place within the universe are divine. We all get what we deserve, no more, no less. Mercy is afforded to those with just hearts and sound minds. Humans devoid of these traits are largely left to fend for themselves. No matter what our external circumstances, no matter what perceptions others around us may have, it is always up to us to reframe any difficulties as potential learning experiences. No suffering on this plane of existence is lacking for purpose.

So lets say for example that your Major Arcana Card is "The World". You may have a very easy-peasy childhood on the outside, but remember that every card has negative attributes of some kind. For further insight, you should look to the meaning of the card's negative attributes along with the definition of its reversed position. This will help you to determine the full picture.

Take time to reflect upon your own darker sides, represented by the cards' reversed position and the negative attributes described. Identify which of these traits do you continually exhibit and which do you deny that you even have. To me, reversals in the Tarot are the equivalent of retrograde natal planets in astrology. When you have retrograde planets in your natal chart, it doesn't mean that those energies are not present within your life, it simply means that you have to work a bit harder to access them. This usually equates to learning spiritual lessons of one kind or another, lessons on how to conduct our lives with a solid set of ethics, boundaries and individualistic purpose. Conquering our own personal challenges helps to unblock these repressed energies within our lives, free up karmic blockages and help get us on a path back towards higher dimensions of universal existence.

The most important part about self-discovery is self-honesty. Until we are honest with ourselves, we will fail to make meaningful internal progress.

Calculating your Rising Sign Cards

Here are your rising sign cards. (This card is for use in your personal depth research or for your client's personal chart and not for use as a card in a 9 card reading).

To find your first Archetypal Court card, look up your baseline sign card.

THE SOUL SYSTEM OF TAROT

Your Rising Sign Card

Signs	Cards
Aries	The Queen of Wands
Taurus	The King of Pentacles
Gemini	The Knight of Swords
Cancer	The Queen of Cups
Leo	The King of Wands
Virgo	The Knight of Pentacles
Libra	The Queen of Swords
Scorpio	The King of Cups
Sagittarius	The Knight of Wands
Capricorn	The Queen of Pentacles
Aquarius	The King of Swords
Pisces	The Knight of Cups

Table 1.2

Above are rising sign court cards; they are based upon traditional western astrological rising signs. They allow you to understand what archetypal personality traits you are presenting to the outside world. This differs from your actual internal personality and thought process, but it will give you a good idea how you relate to others.

The cool thing is that your external persona changes over time due to your progressed chart. People will view you very differently at different points in your life. (Whether you have made progress internally or not is another matter entirely) Even though we maintain the same psychological process, the external way we conduct our day-to-day lives does change, thereby allowing us to grow. At 16 years old, you will experience a vastly different external cycle than what's experienced at 45. And this equates to people responding to you and viewing you in a vastly different manner. This teaches us to work with different types of people: see issues from multiple points of view; balance both our male and female energies. We can then take time out to focus on different life areas such as money, relationships, work, philosophy etc. and learn how to walk in other people's (psychological) shoes. I believe that it is always valuable to understand how people are viewing you at any particular time: it allows you to custom tailor your communicative approach accordingly. This is not an attempt to be manipulative as much is it is an attempt to put your best foot forward.

Suppose you learn that you need to find an astrologer who does advanced progressions work – for this I would recommend contacting myself or another who specializes in progressions work. This will give you an up to the minute update of the external face you are presenting, and even though they are generally 10-12-year transitions (slow moving) they also have 2.75-4 year subsections known as "the decans." The "decans" can give you even more information on how people are responding to you at any given time. I am letting you know you can get as detailed as you like with these kinds of things. For the purposes of this book and for fear of confusing you, I will only cover the basics. Going further than the basics could stifle your desire to learn because the lessons are baffling and difficult without a solid background in the basics.

As an aside, I think it's interesting to note that perhaps infants are so connected because their chart is in full alignment with who they really are, There is a strong connection as to how they view themselves and who they really are. They are in an omnipresent

The Soul System of Tarot

state of being where they experience everything fully with no sense of duality so prevalent in the rest of the world. It is also interesting to note that these cycles take approx. 9-11 years apiece and most spiritual masters don't achieve enlightenment until much later in life. Many of them are over 100 when they are able to finally figure out and transcend the world's duality. These masters have transcended the full cycle of archetypes and are back to where it started in the beginning of their life. In my view Tarot, Astrology and Numerology helps to explain, quite nicely, the phenomenon surrounding these cycles of time.

It is my experience that the progressed rising sign represents an energy that you will be attracting in the outside world during that time as well. For example, when I was in a Queen of Swords progressed rising sign phase many of my clients ended up having this energy running heavily through their charts. It is my opinion that we attract these energy cycles in a bid to learn how to deal with a specific personality type. Personally, I needed to learn how to deal with an unemotional type of feminine energy. And yes there is a difference between male/female and masculine/feminine, which you should also research. I also believe the Princess/Queen of Swords to be the archetypal cards for Los Angeles women, but I digress! This cycle allowed me to learn this archetypal energy's inner workings and to understand that I was attracting these external lessons through my external actions. Perhaps I was also acting emotionlessly on some level and needed to relearn a healthy way to integrate emotional involvement into my day-to-day life. All I can say is that I felt, for one reason or another, it was difficult to trust my heart during this time. I felt very guarded. I hope that you are also able to grasp similar insights concerning the archetypes you are currently facing. I wish I could tell you there were an easy to way to look up your own progressed sign, but you really do need a professional to do that for you. It's that complex.

Let's return to the basic rising signs. The rising sign presents a deeper look at how you present yourself to the outside world and the types of actions that you will use to make a name for yourself or find yourself a suitable occupation/profession etc. In a practical sense you can view it as if it's a filter for your mind; it shows you how you will present yourself to the external world. It shows you how other people will view and respond to your actions. Will you be generally received as being emotional? Logical? Scattered? How will you come off and what can you count on in terms of personal development in these different areas? How can you work to harmonize your external persona with your internal desires? These are all deeper questions that can be aided through the study of these personal rising sign card archetypes.

The Soul System of Tarot

Your Natal Court Cards
(Used In Your Personal Transition Reading)

Designated by Your Month Of Birth...

Your Natal Court Card

Birth Month	Cards
January	The King of Swords
February	The Knight of Cups
March	The Queen of Wands
April	The Knight of Wands
May	The King of Pentacles
June	The Knight of Swords
July	The Queen of Cups
August	The King of Wands
September	The Knight of Pentacles
October	The Queen of Swords
November	The King of Cups
December	The Queen of Pentacles

Table 1.3

These cards represent internal personality struggles within your lifetime. They also serve to reveal more about your internal process and how you generally deal with the life's vagaries. These cards will help you to understand your thought processes, survival mechanisms, social tactics, common forms of self-sabotage, and a host of other things. All of these facets are defined as internal understanding; it's an immensely valuable concept because you realize that you way of thinking is inherently unique to you. When you understand how someone else internally processes an issue, then you can make greater strides towards addressing their issues in a way that's meaningful for them.

Some people are able to do this inherently by picking up on body language and subconscious cues. Others need help with this process. They might be more logically minded and not as emotionally in tune with other people's internal make-up. This is especially true with regards to personal relationships – it's why the book, *Men Are From Mars and Women Are From Venus* was so successful. If you don't know how to communicate with someone on their own terms, then you will be doomed to play out a series of negative relationships. Whereas the previous rising sign was the filter for how you view reality, you can look at this card as your mental engine, so to speak. Are you running on emotional fuel, pure fire, earth energy, or a logical/mental side of life? Although the external struggles will change, the internal personality type is much more fixed. This cycle stays with you for your entire life. It can only be changed if you do serious spiritual developmental work. If this isn't done then the way your mind asserts itself in the external world will pretty much stay the same.

To recap here are things you can look for though analyzing this card:

- Archetypal baseline personality traits
- How people view you externally
- What personality lessons you are subconsciously attracting…

The Soul System of Tarot

At the same time, your base level wiring that dictates how you problem solve or assess challenges will remain pretty fixed. This is the card that you will use at the top of your 9-card reading as a fixed baseline indicator!

This is your permanent natal personality card. This is the card that you will be born under and it will govern the archetypal trials to find personal identity during the beginning of your life. To one degree or another, they will always be present. The thing is that a chart isn't that simple. Just as life is never static, neither are our charts – after all, no human can exist in a void. The good thing is that in life your metaphysical tower can be built as high as you want to go. Remember, the quicker you are able to master your personal human temple, the faster you will acquire freedom in the greater cosmos. The thing about self-mastery is that it is painful – it's why people avoid it. It requires a form of self-demolition and self-sacrifice for higher ideals. It doesn't embrace a comfort driven lifestyle, instead it relies heavily upon a commitment to embracing the world's truth, whatever the cost.

In my experience, the root of freedom lies in spiritual discipline as my good friend Richard King, of the Kings Numerology, always reminds people in his works. Saint Augustine also had a great quote in this regard: "Man has as many masters as he has vices." That pretty much sums it up, if we are able to purify our shadow sides and reinstate a higher level of morality and virtue into our being, there is truly nothing that we cannot achieve.

Secondly, you should look up your rising sign. The rising sign is what you aspire to be like, or aspire to learn at any given phase. The tricky part is that your progressed rising sign actually changes. Your fixed rising sign is a long-term trend you hold on to as a past reference point, but since our rising sign changes, it means that we must also continually master different personality archetypes within our lifetime.

So, to recap, here's what we have. Born rising sign: this can last 2-25 years of time depending on what degree your rising sign is in. There are two ways to figure out where your rising sign is located in your progressed chart: you can either purchase a book on it here – or hire me to compile a chart for you if you do not have the time or energy to compile this information yourself. During our early years these basic archetypal personality traits come largely from our parents and they are by far the strongest archetypes in our lives so they tend to stick with us longer than the phases we go through later in life. I started out as a Knight of Swords Archetypal Gemini. These made up my basic lessons in life, something that was vastly obvious to anyone who went to school with me. Next, my basic rising sign archetype started to kick in late in high school when I decided to figure out what I wanted to do with my professional life. I wanted to be an entrepreneur, which is a total Virgo/Knight of Pentacles archetypal thing to do.

Recently my rising sign changed from Virgo to Libra, which kicked in my Queen of Swords archetype. This transition lessened the psychological importance of making money and instead started to divert my attention to counseling, therapy, and living a truthful life. In later books on this subject, I will describe how these cycles can be divided up even further through the decans. These overarching Archetypes will help you understand the personality types that will come to you to integrate during these time periods.

I remember being mystified when I fell into this new Queen of Swords cycle, as I found literally 40-50% of my female clients were

THE SOUL SYSTEM OF TAROT

drawing these specific court cards during their readings. I thought there was something wrong with me, since I was attracting so much of this sword energy into my life, I felt like there was an overarching lesson I needed to learn from them. And there was: the lesson I needed to learn was that I was in a Swords Cycle.

In the past, I have heard it put it like this: your life's sun sign is what you are destined to achieve. The rising sign presents the skill set you are given to achieve those aims. So, me being a Gemini, I will use the traits of Virgo to achieve that successful Gemini ideal of the speaker/writer/ombudsman. With relation to your chart's archetypal personality development, I find it best to locate your progressed rising sign and use it as your current court card. This informs you as to what lessons you are facing at this time and place. Again, I would like to reference Michael Tsarion's e-book *The Path of the Fool* as a reference work to look this information up in your own readings. Mr. Tsarion has devoted over 30 years of research to the subject. He most definitely possesses a masterful knowledge of the Tarot. I have merely applied this wisdom along with the new way of interpreting readings based upon my own experience in combination with astrology and the greater cycles of time.

Nothing is easy – success has ruined more people than failure. Oddly enough according to the I Ching, the rich man is always in more peril than the poor man. Everyone aims at the person at the top of the hill, while nobody really cares to kick the poor man at the bottom. There is no glory in beating down the poor. Now karmicly speaking it does happen, but the wise thing to do is try our best despite the circumstances we find ourselves in. When we start to realize life's true complexity, we become humbled enough to start making true progress. The ego is little more than the gatekeeper, responsible for keeping us locked away from the entirety of ourselves. It's up to us to metaphorically pass the ego's trials in order for us to rediscover the entirety of ourselves.

Your Hidden Potential/Vocation Card

This card describes your truest, hidden, life-potential. It can point toward many different possible outlets and can manifest in many unconventional forms. During a reading this card is the trickiest because it's not necessarily guaranteed that you will succeed in accessing your true inner power. Utilizing the soul's deep gifts in order to achieve success requires a large personal commitment to personal development and a large time investment. Some people's paths are simpler than others, but this will at least give you a solid direction to follow with regards to what would make you happiest in life. I know some people will say, "well if these cards are based upon the minor arcana, isn't there a good chance that these hidden cards could be overtly negative within their potentiality?" The answer is yes and no. If you draw the three of swords (severe emotional pain) or the 5 of cups (loss of emotional balance and the ending of relationships) and if you were to access these energies in a positive way, you may find yourself involved in a vocation that helps others deal with these severe emotional problems in a meaningful way.

To figure out your hidden potential card, simply add your numerical birth month of with your numerical birth day. Then look at the corresponding table…

The Soul System of Tarot

Number	Cards	Number	Cards	Number	Cards	Number	Cards
1	Ace of Wands	13	3 of Cups	25	5 of Swords	37	7 of Disks
2	2 of Wands	14	4 of Cups	26	6 of Swords	38	8 of Disks
3	3 of Wands	15	5 of Cups	27	7 of Swords	39	9 of Disks
4	4 of Wands	16	6 of Cups	28	8 of Swords	40	10 of Disks
5	5 of Wands	17	7 of Cups	29	9 of Swords		
6	6 of Wands	18	8 of Cups	30	10 of Swords		
7	7 of Wands	19	9 of Cups	31	Ace of Disks		
8	8 of Wands	20	10 of Cups	32	2 of Disks		
9	9 of Wands	21	Ace of Swords	33	3 of Disks		
10	10 of Wands	22	2 of Swords	34	4 of Disks		
11	Ace of Cups	23	3 of Swords	35	5 of Disks		
12	2 of Cups	24	4 of Swords	36	6 of Disks		

Table 1.4 Your Hidden Potential/Vocation Card

Chapter 6

Guide to your vocational potential card!

Here are possible vocational ideas based on your inner desires card. They are merely suggestions but they can point you toward inwardly, fulfilling vocations, whether you cognitively realize it or not. Keep in mind these are just suggestions and your actual career may be vastly different. I merely offer these examples so that you can recognize particular vocational traits which may be similar to some of your existing interests. The "what am I destined to do with my life?" question comes up frequently with many of my clients. I figured that these suggestions would help readers to pursue a productive inner dialogue towards uncovering their vocational answers within. By no means is this an exhaustive list. Quite the contrary, this merely represents a starting point for you to explore more of your internal proclivities and hidden talents.

Suit of Wands

The Suit of the Wands in the Minor Arcana are synonymous with the great action hero of the deck. They represent fire, so they will always inherently crave action and attention, along with being masters of getting out of a tight spot. "When in doubt, burn your way out" might be a good motto for these cards. Fire is a transmutational substance; as such it cannot be boxed in or easily contained. Fire is the most passionate out of all of the elements, which can make it the most impulsive as well.

It's always good to guard your heart when you are dealing with this archetype because in your haste for victory you may rush into things that are not good for you long term. If you fall under this heading you should also try to cultivate personal centering and calming rituals of some kind. This will help channel the anger in your life, allowing you to fight the evils within yourself and the world. Passion is fine, but just like a wildfire, it can quickly become uncontrollable if you allow it too much room to burn. No matter what, you should always embrace an action-oriented doer type mentality. You are a representative for taking real-world action. So a sedentary lifestyle may not work out for you. The fire within could start to burn you from the inside out.

Ace of Wands

The Ace of Wands is a card of intense energy and action. It inspires heroic efforts of every shade. It allows you to draw a deep inner potential from the universe's raw, creative energy. People will be inspired by your will to action along with your propensity for not taking no for an answer. Even though situations may often end in arguments, you are generally able to be a catalyst of positive change when channeling your energies correctly. For an Ace of Wands person life is a roller coaster – they are usually up front and center, looking to enter the fray and make a statement in some way. It's not the most public card, but perhaps it's the most driven. For you to remain healthy and happy this card requires tons of physical activity. At bare minimum walking for 30 minutes a day will help your demeanor and serve to provide you with some peace of mind. It's also a good idea to retire into nature from time to time to restore your great fiery energies and rebalance your inner sense of calm. Lao Tzu said, "the world is won by those who let go, for those who try and try the world is beyond winning". Moral of the story being: there's a time for action and a time to step back and let the world fix itself. Careers that might suit you include: pioneer, explorer, athlete, martial artist, manual laborer, gardener, construction worker, general contractor, union organizer, peoples champion, human rights advocate, industrial planner, stuntman, race car driver, publicist.

Negative

You may experience times where you slip into a less productive mode, a mode where you question the overarching meaning behind existence. If it is only for a few days, this is fine. However, an Ace of Wands person should never be sitting still, especially if they have a surplus of baseline primal energy that needs to be exerted. It's like leaving a fire burning alone for too long, sooner or later something else always ignites. You are responsible for managing your internal energy source. If you want to contemplate life, find an activity such as meditation or martial arts that allows you to channel this energy in a different manner. Be warned – you do not want to waste this precious wellspring of internal fortitude with which you have been blessed. Leadership might take time for you to develop, but be patient – poor leadership often results in bad karma. Remember not to avoid your spiritual responsibility to yourself. You are the custodian of your soul; to do less than your best is to disrespect your own higher self. For most people in today's society lack of effort is the true nature of sin. They disrespect themselves to a far greater degree than they would ever disrespect others.

These are some careers that you might try if your not living up to your true potential: sex worker, exotic dancer, soldier, assassin, stunt person or a military contractor.

Dates associated with this card

October 31st, November 30th, December 29th.

"A leader is best when people barely know he exists, when his work is done, his aim fulfilled, they will say: we did it ourselves."

-Lao Tzu

2 of Wands

On it's high side, this is an archetypal, intuitive, decision-maker card. You are enabled to make decisions on the fly that would make most other people's heads spin for months. This is a profound talent that needs to be channeled into an activity that forces you to trust yourself and your deeper inner answers. This is also a card for those who like to have multiple projects going on at any one time. You are also capable of going into a situation to mix things up when need be. This is a supremely dynamic archetype and can make the cultivation of personal relationships a paramount asset in your long-term success. To a large extent the 2 card rules close partnerships and camaraderie. Perhaps you would enjoy being a personal

The Soul System of Tarot

assistant, project manager or any role with many different responsibilities that allows freewheeling and keeping professional options open. Perhaps you will like power behind the throne positions such as a producer, trading specialist, director, artisan merchant, sales, marketing, client relations, PR, event design or project management. Anything that forces you to use your exemplary intuitive snap judgments would be a good choice. When coupled with spiritual activities that allow further personal development and that translates into a recipe for success. Having faith in your own intuitive decision-making process is a vital key to professional success; indecision leads to personal failure. Your motto could be: "it's better to make the wrong decision than no decision at all!"

Negative

An inability to make decisions about your career and not trusting intuition are sure signs that you're not yet living up to your full potential. This is an example of how your greatest weakness can become your greatest strength. All you need is time and faith in yourself. Perhaps at life's outset you lack trust in your own innate abilities or you just crack under pressure. Maybe you feel uncomfortable juggling many different tasks or you are scattered at work due to your extracurricular pursuits. You could also suffer from pursuing a highly external lifestyle that allows you to avoid making firm decisions about your spiritual life. You might also have a hard time figuring out internal motivations. Many times these motivations are subconscious. Concerning your own life, this forces you to become a detective and realize the importance of decoding your mind's the inner workings. Be on guard for a lack of professionalism. Also you may have a tendency to attract problem business partners who move too fast in projects, thereby sacrificing quality. It may be easier to work for someone else until you work out the quirks of your own unique business approach. Since this is a 2 card you would do well to incorporate a partnership or other working-group style cooperation.

Dates associated with this card

January 1st, November 31st, December 30th.

> *Some of our important choices have a time line. If we delay a decision, the opportunity is gone forever. Sometimes our doubts keep us from making a choice that involves change. Thus an opportunity may be missed.*
>
> *James E. Faust*

3 of Wands

At day's end, the 3 of Wands archetypes are best when functioning to cultivate a firm sense of camaraderie in any cooperative effort. Rolling solo isn't a passion of yours, although it can be if you are planning, in some way, activities for others. If nothing else, you enjoy helping others from afar. Financial planning and other forms of personal assistance would also work well. Working philanthropically for a non-profit organization or volunteering on different committees would also help you progress. Ultimately you are looking to experience many different management scenarios or other creative ways to navigate interpersonal leadership and development. Possible careers include: managers, agents,

THE SOUL SYSTEM OF TAROT

contractors, team builders, motivational speakers, leadership counselors, resource allocation management, conductors, athletes, project management, supervisors, efficiency experts, consultants, life coaches, networking specialists, social media managers, event promoters, sports coaches, script supervising or city planning would all be good options for you.

Negative side

On the downside, it may take years to come to a full understanding of your dynamic, leadership potential. You may shy away from the management roles in an attempt to play it safe and go along to get along. You may hold back some of your own unique personal development energy in an attempt to gain others approval. The strange thing about approval is that if you just do your own thing and march to the beat of your own drummer, then you often naturally stumble upon acceptance. Even the most oddball artists and extreme personalities eventually find a sense of worldly well adjustment, (given they have some spiritual grounding and are free from drug problems). You will eventually attract people who are inspired by your strong sense of self. Otherwise you are stuck becoming a follower and stuck modifying your life to fit in with the pack and be "normal". Here is a news flash for you: "normal" doesn't exist on this planet. Everyone has problems, but people are either striving to become better or striving to stay the same. There's not much "normal" happening as far as I can tell. Don't lose faith in your greater vision of your own life and realize that we all need help on some level to accomplish our grander visions. No man is an island, so don't be afraid of team potentialities.

Austin Muhs

Dates associated with this card

January 2nd, February 1st, December 31st.

Everyone suffers some injustice in life, and what better motivation than to help others not suffer in the same way.

Bella Thorne

4 of Wands

Creating systems based on day-to-day structure is natural for you. It's most important to analyze how to keep things happening in a spirit of harmonious cooperation. You could also work to pioneer new cultural holidays, awards ceremonies, or other ritualistic events. This could also be a hidden skill of yours and humanity always needs a reason to celebrate the spiritual dynamic of personal accomplishment – finding a way to facilitate this could be right up your alley. Perhaps you could learn things from other tribal or ancient societal structures and help to integrate them into a helpful modern day context. I think we can all agree that the form of cultural life and societal governance available to us today is lacking to say the least. Some subsections of the populace still have some form of community, but by and large America has become the "melting pot" of a dog-eat-dog lifestyle. One thing is certain, everyone is looking out for number one. Perhaps you could work towards fixing this in some way. If nothing else, you should work on serving as a positive cultural role model for others.

Possible vocational options include being a city planner, dispatcher, route coordinator, event planner, promoter, property manager, programming project coordinator, architectural planner, race team captain, life coaching, team builder, community workspace coordinator or anything in the health and wellness field could work for you as well.

Negative

On the negative side you could become a scatterbrained employee who just sucks at their job. Being ineffectual at work is common for people who are not following their true passion. Sometimes it's a form of self-sabotage: making mistakes at work can cause problems, showing you that you're on the wrong track. Other times you "really just don't care" to paraphrase Peter from the movie *Office Space*. Just remember that you have to earn your dream job, nobody is going to hand it to you. This process involves much personal sacrifice in order to eventually obtain your goals. In my opinion, sacrifice is the best weapon we have against life's uncertainties. What we willingly give up can no longer control us. The more we give up, the more we naturally receive. The more we can give up, then the less we have to lose. There are strange paradoxes in the universe. It is also important to note that the ability to delay gratification is one of the only thing separating humans from total barbarism and chaos. If we cannot delay our desires, then we don't deserve to have said experiences in the first place. Don't be afraid to ask others for help; especially if they are more experienced in certain areas, this allows you to move forward in a well thought out manner. Second opinions are never a bad idea, even if you think you have a solid idea of what to do. An outside perspective usually works to foster foresight and can act as a devils advocate to your plans.

Austin Muhs

Dates associated with this card

January 3rd, February 2nd, March 1st.

> *Guided by nothing but pop culture values, many children no longer learn how to think about morality and virtue, or to think of them at all. They grow up with no shared moral framework, believing that the highest values are diversity, tolerance and non-judgmentalism.*
>
> Gary Bauer

5 of Wands

This is a very competitive and antagonistic card. This is for those who are happiest mixing it up amongst the fray. Perhaps you would be interested in direct one-on-one competition in your professional life. Perhaps you would enjoy being a salesperson, attorney, community activist, athlete, industrialist, statesman, politician, industry disruptor, inventor, a professional martial artist or fighter, conflict arbiter, or even a middle manager. Whatever you do, the ability to steer the middle ground is paramount for your long-term success. You, also, have a deep desire to stay "in the mix" no matter the outcome. Being in the mix is a good thing, but remember not to define yourself by constant struggle. That would merely represent your role inside the war, instead of identifying with the warrior who at some stage is able to transcend that struggle.

I believe we all know people who are addicted to conflict in their personal relationships; if you're not careful this can also happen with you in your choice of careers. You need to make sure and define yourself as the person who creates harmony out of conflict, not seeking conflict for it's own sake. A prime example of this was Steve Jobs, a person who actively welcomed conflicts with those who had differing opinions within his organization. He was tyrannical in his management style, but obviously this style worked for him and the organization he represented. Sadly I believe that it also eventually cost him his health. Ensnaring yourself in mental warfare eventually takes its toll on the body; the external war starts to manifest itself internally as well. Remember the old maxim "As above, so below" it applies to us as well. Everything has a price. If you are out of harmony with the universe, the universe will always find a way to let you know. These wake up calls can come in many different forms.

Negative

Beware of choosing poor partnerships problematic teammates. They can cause long-term headaches if your not careful. You may also attract professions which places you in a position to use clout to manipulate others sexual energy. This is never advised. You need to trust yourself. Don't overwork yourself, it will not help anyone. Conflict for it's own sake is useless and represents a karmic loop you have failed to conquer. Life is filled with challenge, however, a smart person picks their battles and is never consumed by the conflict. There is a famous parable about a man who followed around Shakyamuni Buddha for three days berating and cursing at him. After three days the man was frustrated, as he could not anger the Buddha. The man finally asked him, "Why are you not getting mad, I have been yelling at you for days?" Shakyamuni replied, "Your anger is a gift that I choose not to receive." This is a good parable concerning an individual and conflict. Conflict may follow you around in one form or another – it's your choice whether or not

Austin Muhs

to accept conflict's energetic complications.

Dates associated with this card

January 4th, February 3rd, March 2nd, April 1st.

I am at peace with God. My conflict is with Man.

Charlie Chaplin

6 of Wands

Perhaps the most public of all of the vocational cards, this card would indicate that commandeering leadership roles and or being in the limelight are of utmost importance to your long-term happiness. That being said, it's always a good idea to be careful what you wish for. Perhaps you will enjoy becoming an actor, politician, musician, independent mogul of some sort, community leader, general, PR specialist, an athlete, a company figurehead, spokesperson, radio announcer, DJ, TV anchor, model, voiceover artist or a peoples champion. Virtually anything that puts you in the public eye or lands you with a leadership role would likely make you happiest. Take your professional image seriously because losing public respect would be a huge blow to your ego; your sense of self is often intimately tied to your career. This archetype should use their public role to benevolently affect others and become a legitimate voice for society's voiceless, not another ego freak. The world needs people who use their personal internal struggle to help change the world for the better. People will always be available to support you, but only if you are there to support their dreams. If you always put your spiritual life first then you have no need for concern; life will always

The Soul System of Tarot

balance out when you understand that this reality is by no means the end-all-be-all of existence. It is merely a place of learning and if we are lucky we can garner some deeper understanding into the inner workings of the universe.

Negative

I believe that the downside here would be that you are in danger of becoming in love with yourself or your career. If you cannot develop a strong spiritual compass or derive an internal sense of approval and self worth, then you may be stuck chasing after the ever-elusive heights of fame and fortune. Fame is an unquenchable thirst, just like the sufferings of power and greed. You can experience these things without understanding the deeper underlying spiritual connotations of their usefulness. At this point, I would advise you to halt all activities and reflect until you have a firm understanding of your deeper purpose. Superficiality always ends at some point. Often it ends poorly for the ego. Ego is left holding the bag – ego was most likely the culprit of your personal misfortune arising from a lack of deeper purpose. This situation is not trivial. In my opinion it comes with a definite measure of danger. The world is filled with envious people who can end up causing problems if you are not maintaining humble and philanthropic intentions. Virtue always helps to keep you safe; throwing your weight around or indulging ego will always attract destruction. Obviously, for this card archetype, vanity and narcissism are indicators of being on the wrong path, so user beware! The Tao Te Ching advises: "accomplish what needs to be accomplished for the good of the world and move on". The sage does not dwell on accomplishments or rest on laurels. This only attracts long-term envy, spite, and disrepute. As difficult as it may seem, let accomplishments pass through you, don't identify or grasp onto them. Pride is always present at the beginning of any fall from personal or professional grace.

Dates associated with this card

January 5th, February 4th, March 3rd, April 2nd, May 1st.

> *The one characteristic of authentic power that most people overlook is humility. It is important for many reasons. A humble person walks in a friendly world. He or she sees friends everywhere he or she looks, wherever he or she goes, whomever he or she meets. His or her perception goes beyond the shell of appearance and into essence.*
>
> *Gary Zukav*

7 Of Wands

I believe that this represents the archetypal spiritual warrior card. It is a lone wolf (7 energy), which won't make compromise or take flak from anyone. With this energy you would probably be happiest as some form of rebel or societal disruptor. It might not be the easiest path that you have chosen, but the internal rewards you can harvest from this path are immense. In the grander scheme of things, we are only here for a limited portion of time. Taken into perspective you may understand that despite drawing a challenging mission, you can recognize the shortness of your assignment. I believe that writing is also a perfect profession for you. They say that the pen is mightier than the sword. Perhaps you can work towards changing the world

The Soul System of Tarot

with your verbal abilities. A spiritual leadership role of some sort may also be a good fit. Finding periods of repose in nature or teaching ethics or other moral discernment modalities to young people, will help feed your soul. You may enjoy fasting, becoming a comedian, a social innovator who finds new ways to harmonize human life via reforming societal structures. These archetypes always tend to steer towards the paths less trodden and find pleasure in standing up for what's right. They seek justice, balance and harmony. Any trade possessing these traits is a natural home for the 7 of Wands personage.

Negative

On the negative side you may be running away from the gravity of your spiritually directed vocational tasks: taking the easy way out, hiding away in corporate America somewhere. This is a personal recipe for disaster because anytime 7 energy runs away, bad things happen. Bad things: addiction, depression, superficiality, loss of center, attracting self-sabotage in your working life or being dealt with by uncaring or callous characters out in the "real" world. Any of these unfortunate events are possible if you are shirking your spiritual responsibility to yourself and to the planet at large. Trust me, I have done some shirking in my day and it made my life a living hell, (I have some seven energy in my chart). You also have the propensity for making yourself a martyr, or painting yourself into a corner. People always want someone to blame, but there's no glory in falling on your own sword. You can't lead many people if you get yourself locked up. Most times its best to lead silently, for talk is cheap. Only a fool runs his mouth in a feeble attempt to reform society with his vocal cords alone. Societal reform creeps in silently from the void of your spiritual center. As you purify your mind, so does the world start to purify itself around you. Such changes are truly divine in nature. So instead of thoughtlessly hitting the panic button, figure out how to lead through a form of spiritual osmosis. I understand it seems challenging, but I believe it is possible. Silence isn't quite as quiet as we might think…

Dates associated with this card

January 6th, February 5th, March 4th, April 3rd, May 2nd, June 1st.

> *"Be careful in dealing with a man who cares nothing for comfort or promotion, but is simply determined to do what he believes to be right. He is a dangerous uncomfortable enemy, because his body, which you can always conquer, gives you little purchase upon his soul."*
>
> *Gilbert Murray*

8 of Wands

This card always puts you smack dab in the fray. A high-speed or high-pressure profession is perfect for you. You will thrive in any occupation that forces you to work on a deadline: journalism, racing (of all forms), and sales. Businesses that deal primarily with women might be fulfilling. Running a small business or some other form of startup would work splendidly as well. These professions put you neck deep in the action. On a more pragmatic level. you could run a moving company. You could work in some form of transportation, perhaps as a truck driver or other schedule motivated career. You could also be: a stock trader, a railroad worker, a transportation specialist, an aviator, a debater, a comedian, a shipping executive, a

The Soul System of Tarot

venture capitalist or a teacher. Whatever you choose, you need to work hard towards completing a specific set of short medium term objectives. You can't rely on the world to motivate you. You have to figure out ways to get passionate and get moving on your own. As Micahael Tsarion puts it, "it's not life's job to give you meaning, it's your job to give meaning to life". You seem to naturally understand the processes behind many of today's modern workflows'. Corporate America will recognize your proficiency at achieving results smoothly and quickly. Business consulting, logistics event coordination and transportation management are all solid options as well.

Negative

The card's negative virtues include compulsive gambling, extreme sports, being a mercenary, dealing with heavy machinery, disregarding safety practices, taking needless risks, rushing things, not taking proper precautions, gun running, and dealing with all kinds of weapons in general. Because you enjoy the fast life, living life in the fast lane can have its own set of dangers and drawbacks. It's fine to want to go fast, as long as your not headed headlong into a karmic brick wall. Remember that Lao Tzu stated, "Nature never rushes, yet everything gets accomplished!"

Dates associated with this card

January 7th, February 6th, March 5th, April 4th, May 3rd, June 2nd, July 1st.

All action results from thought, so it is thoughts that matter.

Sai Baba

Austin Muhs

9 of Wands

With the 9 of wands we begin to deal with a more warrior type archetype, someone who refuses to take no for an answer. At their best they will battle life's obstacles until the bitter end and achieve their aims through a sheer effort of will. As the saying goes: "the harder you work, the luckier you get". This card makes it utterly impossible to shrink from your life challenges without suffering severe depression. Nobody likes a quitter. With this as your personal dream card, you can't afford to quit on your dreams. The 9 of wands is all about the active struggle and how fighting and winning the good fight makes you happier in the long run. It's hard to say exactly how difficult your chart will be without taking into consideration your other static personal cards, but no matter what the obstacle you will be tested to the extreme before you reach your mark. Persistence is the key with this card. If you continue working you will eventually succeed. More often than not, you will do so in a sustainable way.

Tuning into higher spiritual guidance can be a tedious process, but it is extremely important that you make the attempt. Internal guidance is a great secret weapon to have when you feel like something is off in your life. Trying too hard at vocations or professions that lack a long-term, sense of purpose will lead you nowhere. Remember, Rome wasn't built in a day. This restart process occurs due to a lack of faith or self trust at key junctures in your career decision-making process.

Career paths you might like include: entrepreneurial work, construction, architectural design, endurance sports, animal husbandry, electrical work, firefighting, and being a paramedic, basically anything that requires you to push yourself and is driven by higher purpose. Lighting or movie production work might also hold a special interest for you. You won't reach fulfillment unless you are truly exerting yourself on a day-to-day basis!

Negative

Watch out for people who would steal your ideas or other intellectual property. Procrastinating: beware of looking too short-term when planning out your vocational life. Avoid half-hearted attempts at projects or other work related communications. Never give up on yourself or your plans in mid-stream. Work on seeing them through till the end. Avoid being drawn into another's low moral behavior patterns. Always maintain a high sense of self despite any setbacks. Remember the tortoise eventually beats the hare every time. Peaking too early can also qualify as a negative event. Never worry about conquering projects or career goals merely for the sake of recognition or peer approval. If you don't possess a true spiritually derived overarching motive you are in danger of having a lackluster career. You have to let established methods go and do your own thing if you want to thrive in this archetype. Deep down you want to work hard so embrace a meaningful methodology when taking action.

Dates associated with this card

January 8th, February 7th, March 6th, April 5th, May 4th, June 3rd, July 2nd, August 1st.

> *I love those who can smile in trouble, who can gather strength from distress, and grow brave by reflection. 'Tis*

Austin Muhs

the business of little minds to shrink, but they whose heart is firm, and whose conscience approves their conduct, will pursue their principles unto death.

Leonardo da Vinci

10 of Wands...

Remember, when it's too tough for everyone else it's just right for the 10 of wands. Anything extreme applies here, stunt driving, martial arts, fighting, survivalist training, search and rescue, competition weight lifters, illusionists, fire jumpers, all of these professions would be well suited to a 10 of wands. You could also box, become a small business owner, entrepreneur, inventor, visionary, spiritual monk or spiritual ascetic. It's important that whatever you do, you attempt to find something that harnesses the vast reserves of your internal energy. You thrive when you view your life as a courageous war. Every day you awaken ready to take arms in a new battle. If you enjoy your feminine you look into doing personal training, structural artistry, botany, husbandry, gardening. Consider pursuing things that take a long time to master but that you eventually become such an expert that others approach you for advice. Awakening early and maintaining a tight schedule works to help build a solid framework for long-term success. Gluttony can also be an issue for this card. Wanting it all sometimes translate to wanting too much food as well. Luckily these urges are usually emotionally rooted urges that can be corrected sustainably through holistic means.

The Soul System of Tarot

Negative side

The downside here is that you may want to hold the entire world in your hands. From my personal experience this is an archetype that makes people want everything in the world to be perfect and "just so". When we step back and analyze our lives, I think everyone can say that most things they fervently believed would come true probably took longer to materialize then they originally hoped. Some times goals have taken goal seekers on a completely different route to success then first visualized. Whatever the factors, the key here is to honestly assess your overall life expectations. You may never have it all. If you are one of those rare creatures who end up living a successful fairy tale life, then it usually means that you had to give up a hell of a lot to get there. Generally speaking nothing in this world is free. You either pay in blood sweat, tears, or karma. Nobody eats for free! Nobody knows this better than a hard-working 10 of wands archetype driven to accomplish the impossible when it is in line with their highest dharma alignment.

Hard work may seem exhausting. Spiritual work is a Catch-22. It ends up being a "tired if you do, unhappy if you don't" situation. If you don't whole-heartedly apply yourself towards your passions, then you may end up with feelings of regret and self-hatred. Then you will start to beat yourself up because you just know that you are doing injustice to the motives of your higher spiritual self. You become your own worst critic. You become real friendly with the words shoulda,' woulda,' and coulda'. So I say: to heck with that! Just freaking go for it! I've heard it said: there is plenty of time to sleep when you are dead. Throw caution to the wind and create that passionate life that you thought was only possible for others. If you are helping the world be better, then the world will help you to be better as well.

Dates associated with this card

January 9th, February 8th, March 7th, April 6th, May 5th, June 4th, July 3rd, August 2nd, September 1st.

> *There is only one day left, always starting over: it is given to us at dawn and taken away from us at dusk.*
>
> Jean-Paul Sartre

Suit of Cups

If your inner fulfillment card falls within the suit of the cups, then that means that some form of emotionality or personal emotional development will be a major key in finding a sense of accomplishment and peace of mind during this lifetime. Try not to be dependent upon external results for your innate happiness. For the cups, the deepest fulfillment in life lives on the emotional level. You can get what you want out of life through internal feelings, not the external accouterments. The most important thing I would say is that cups people should never stagnate. Cups people always need to be in motion, even if that motion is at a very moderate pace. You need to identify the things in life that help your emotionality flow through you. You can be quite the unhappy camper when your emotions sit and fester for too long. Obviously this is not a free ticket to indulge your anger or sadness, but you need to be actively engaging with the world in emotionally meaningful ways. Perhaps you should consider doing self-developmental work in the form of journaling or a similar creative endeavor. Music starts and ends with the people of the cups who really love to engage with life on this surreal auditory level.

It's important that you take your creative life seriously – for you, it's a life necessity. If you are not actively engaging your emotions through creative or caregiving ways, then you will feel like something is missing in your life and you will not know what to do to fill the void. Be good to yourself and embrace your potentials as a universal muse. People need to be inspired, even if sometimes it's in an overly dramatic fashion. Without that emotional release, people would be stuck in their heads, crunching numbers and pushing pencils, and letting go of their innate forms of compassion. We all know these types: people who haven't cried in years and have instead chose to shut off their emotions and repress the pain in their life. I think that human beings all know and understand that this is not a healthy way of dealing with emotions. It's actually a cup's responsibility to evoke that meaningful reaction from the other suits. Because if a cup doesn't do it, who else will?

Sadly, this suit brings a lot of internal angst and sadness along for the ride, but without sorrow happiness might not feel as euphoric. Remember not to attach to the emotions but instead try your best to let them pass right through you. If you adopt this philosophy, your sensitivity can then become your strength. Water is fluid and ever changing. As such, your desires may feel like they are fluid and ever changing. This is because they will be. For you, life fulfillment doesn't depend on the destination as much as it does on the journey's emotional involvement. The aim here isn't to bottle up the water, or to make it subservient to your aims, it's to let the water flow through you and take you where it want's you to go. Keep the following passage of the Tao Te Ching in mind when you are considering your vocational destiny.

> "Under heaven nothing is more soft and yielding than water.
>
> Yet for attacking the solid and strong, nothing is better;
>
> It has no equal.
>
> The weak can overcome the strong;
>
> The supple can overcome the stiff.
>
> Under heaven everyone knows this,
>
> Yet no one puts it into practice."
>
> Tao Te Ching - Lao Tzu - chapter 78

Ace of Cups

This card is the quintessential emotional instigator. Someone who is able to channel the vast reserves of their being and transmute that beautiful spiritual energy into things that others can enjoy. If this is your card, you have a deep need to channel your vast emotional resources into some emotional endeavor. You become an emotional pillar for all of those around you. Whatever brings emotional growth is a great career choice for you. Your capacity to openly use your heart to care (notice I didn't say love) for others is what matters. Love is a difficult term to define in a modern context and represents a more fleeting sense of rapture than a sustainable reverence for another human being. Whenever you hear the word

The Soul System of Tarot

love, I would always remember that actions speak louder than words. Care, on the other hand, frequently stands up to the test of time.

As an Ace of Cups, you have a deep need to show the world your true colors through meaningful emotional interactions. This represents a very motherly archetype or energy where you are able to help others work out their own emotional foibles. However, first and foremost, you should work on healing yourself.

This card may point you towards having a family and family life, but remember if you are not 100 percent certain of marriage success then you may want to forgo this experience. You may get stuck in emotionally draining encounters, robbing you of spiritual energy. When you're married much energy is expended toward solving someone else's problems. We all want to make progress and eventually evolve past the need for this difficult dimension, known as earth. Exerting all of your energy into relationships means that there is very little time left over which to accomplish such goals.

You have the capacity to lead a rich and rewarding emotional life. You should definitely use this in either an artistic or a healing capacity. Any one of the creative arts would satisfy your desires, along with helping others conquer their own emotional problems. Careers to consider: dancer, stay at home mother, (I don't say father because it's bad Feng Shui for men to spend too much time at home) dream analyst, healer, doctor, acupuncturist, massage therapist, hypnotist, veterinarian, writer, painter, counselor, psychologist, philosopher, artist, actor, comedian, performer, magician, director, film maker. Basically you should look to any career that allows you to connect to others on a 1-to-1 level.

Austin Muhs

Negative

The hard part about the Ace of Cups is that, for various reasons, your heart might be shut down by the time you reach adulthood. All it takes is a few relationships gone badly, or a few people who make you feel emotionally inadequate, and you then shut down your heart. Then it can take years of spiritual development and/or personal healing work before you learn to trust your heart again. This can considerably delay vocational progress. In life there are no Archimedean points where everything is going to be perfect and you can integrate your healing process into your day-to-day vocational life. You just have to make it happen despite whatever else is happening in your life. We must remember not to neglect our own healing as spiritual beings amongst the myriad of other responsibilities and day-to-day activities. If you neglect your own healing you might be prone to emotional breakdown or long-term depression. Also you need to focus on boundaries, boundaries, and boundaries, because there's a time to help and a time to reserve your personal energy. If you don't learn this lesson early, you are going to have a long series of codependent interactions before you finally wake up. Your aim is to help others live life but not at the expense of you living your own life.

Dates associated with this card

January 10th, February 9th, March 8th, April 7th, May 6th, June 5th, July 4th, August 3rd, September 2nd, October 1st.

> *I think that beauty can injure you to death. It can cause an injury that can never be cured. Or it can so traumatize you, your life changes direction. The beauty of*

The Soul System of Tarot

the harmony of nature that is forever lost, or a daily rite that you perform, or diving into the sea for a swim. Those experiences are going to mark you.

Toni Servillo

2 of Cups

It does not get more romantic or love oriented than the vocational disposition of the 2 of Cups. Perhaps you are eternally questing for that one true romance or never ending love affair. Or perhaps you are more interested in a comfortable life, filled with friends, family and a secure existence. Perhaps you would enjoy being a cruise ship director, managing an exotic hotel somewhere or taking your life into your own hands through some form of friendship building. On the other side you could be great at childcare, being a PTA leader, community organizer, chef or landscape architect amongst other things. Whatever you do with this card your focus should be on smaller personal relationship groups. The 2 of cups is all about the personal relationship sphere.

On a more corporate level perhaps you could work with businesses to open up lines of emotional communication in the workplace. Corporations are swiftly changing due to the new wave of startups. Careers in conflict resolution, relationship counseling, and legal arbitration might all be good. All kinds of relationship facilitation type roles would be superb for you. Perhaps you want to sing about love as a lounge singer. Even though love is just a word, (and a loosely defined word at that) it really becomes a profound vehicle of compassion when you talk about the personal 1-to-1 type care that you can extend to others with this 2 of cups archetype!

Selling jewelry or working in event planning might be a good fit for you. Building meaningful friendships and connections with others of like mind is important for your personal development.

Negative

On the card's dark side, you could be a hopeless love addict. You could refuse to do any personal work, or face any type of isolation that bars you from building a solid sense of self. Instead you may be running headlong from one bad relationship to another, wondering why you keep attracting the same types of assholes. The problem is that your internal sense of self is being defined by your personal relationships and not by who you really are and how you are contributing to your own personal spiritual development.

Time is something you never get back. If you're about to spend time on someone, you need to be damn well sure that that someone is worth every bit of energy that you are expending. If not, then you are sacrificing your spiritual self at their behest. Nobody values a self-sacrificing martyr. If you make yourself overly available, due to a lack of boundaries, somebody will invariably come along to use you. You need boundaries to avoid the dark side of a torrid personal life.

As a brief aside, these types of troubled personal relationships can always come in the form of personal family issues as well, although that's a bit less likely (not being able to see your full chart makes it difficult to say). For you, love is either really good or really bad. It can color your life either way. Other people may be able to focus on work or other areas. For you ,relationships can be a bit all consuming.

The Soul System of Tarot

Dates associated with this card

January 11th, February 10th, March 9th, April 8th, May 7th, June 6th, July 5th, August 4th, September 3rd, October 2nd, November 1st.

Being deeply loved by someone gives you strength, while loving someone deeply gives you courage.

Lao Tzu

3 of cups

This is an archetypal card of celebration: events, parties, engagements, honor giving festivities, birthdays, weddings, anything that allows people to come together in commemoration applies here. Perhaps you would enjoy wedding planning, event planning, coordinating or scheduling recreational activities, or being a talent scout. The key is to find something that brings people together and honors life. To celebrate is to understand the true gravity of time cycles happening within our lives. When reverentially utilized, celebration creates a sense of harmony, cooperation and most importantly reinforcement for noble virtues within the human race.

Today, sadly, most humans celebrations fall in the "celebrate because it's Friday" category. This does little more than serve to reinforce your addiction to the status quo. Finding meaningful ways to help people break this paradigm is effectively reinventing the culture and is a great way for you to spend your vocational efforts. Life is hard. People need a way to understand that others are there to alleviate the burden by sharing in their struggles and triumphs. Cultural events are one of the best ways of accomplishing just such tasks. They can come together to commemorate life's poignant events. It's hard to say how far any of us will go in life, but at the end of the day there will have been many different people who have helped us to get where we are going. We are merely men (or women) "standing on the shoulders of giants", as Isaac Newton so aptly put it. The more you learn about the world, the more you come to realize that there is truly nothing new under the sun. When you truly own this philosophy then life becomes truly focused on personal evolution rather than external evolution, simply because true, creative, life work is accomplished within.

Negative

On the negative side, you could trend towards indulging your hedonistic side with alcohol or drugs or whatever substances are in vogue in the party lifestyle. This tendency towards overt extroversion or escapism needs to be eradicated from your life as quickly as possible. The sooner you learn how to cultivate internal happiness instead of expecting it to come from outside, the happier you will be. Perhaps you personally find that it's easier and more productive to maintain a strictly intoxicant free lifestyle. I have lived this way myself for quite some time and I personally dig it. Even though for some there are transcendent usages for drugs and alcohol, I would imagine that any instances of this happening in the day-to-day world are exceedingly rare. Having smoked weed for years and been a party addict in my past, I have to say that I am much happier and much more emotionally stable now due to my reformed lifestyle. On the other hand I am a coffee addict, which is still an actual addiction. I find it hard to believe that coffee will be killing me anytime soon. Nor will coffee be altering my sense of good judgment. It will not tamper with my internal emotional

The Soul System of Tarot

disposition. I think a tight leash should be kept on the pleasure-oriented activities so prevalent for this archetype; it can get you into trouble later on…!

Dates associated with this card

January 12th, February 11th, March 10th, April 9th, May 8th, June 7th, July 6th, August 5th, September 4th, October 3rd, November 2nd, December 1st.

> If art is to nourish the roots of our culture, society must set the artist free to follow his vision wherever it takes him.
>
> John F. Kennedy

4 of Cups

This is the quintessential positive card. It embraces you with deep insight and vision into your long-term sense of self. It allows you to easily discern what you ultimately want for your life. The only difficulty is having the patience to wait it out. Succinctly put: understanding life's higher aspirations is extremely difficult but if this is your archetypal card then patience is your strong point, making it easier to patiently overcome life's obstacles and seeing your higher aspirations reach fruition. To vigorously pursue life's goals it is best to move methodically while waiting with a calm sense of acceptance. Rushing recklessly ahead usually results into a quick, mad dash to failure. In the cosmic sense, life gives us more time to succeed. Some high masters forgo all form of external "success" in this realm in order to achieve a higher form of success in the next realm, wherever that may be. These meditative masters are not stupid men. They know that this world isn't the end all be all. These masters believe that there are many worlds out in the cosmos and many other dimensions outside of this one. It will probably take time for you to believe this but there are people who routinely visit these places in their mind. These people have the dedication to abstain from the world's karmic potholes. They realize that the earth is not their final stop. Consequently they have dedicated themselves to something higher – unharnessing man's true potential. You can do this also but only if you choose to do so.

To sum it up: this archetype's rewards are the possessions of inexhaustible levels of patience and an uncanny introspective ability. It gives ample room to work from within so the external world's negative voice is muted. The cool thing about the imagination is that, in a sense, you can instantly have anything you want. Some may call it daydreaming, others call it meditation. Whatever your chosen path, keep in mind that there are many spiritual mountains to climb: only those with supreme heart and untold discipline will reach the peak of their own universal potential. Perhaps you wish to set out upon that quest? Perhaps guiding other toward a sense of internal serenity will make you happier. Remember, emotional stability is a major part of your vocational quest no matter what you choose to pursue.

Negative side

Impatience is your downfall. Remember that the greatest threat of failure lies right before success. If you are not able to really embody your true, career purpose right off the bat, just remember to be patient. Life has a funny way of utilizing a roundabout route in order to place us where we need to be, as long as we keep the faith (keeping the faith being the hard part, naturally). I also believe that if you cannot maintain a solid emotional center in your chosen career then you may want to ask yourself if that career is really for you.

With this archetype you should really be able to master your emotions by the end of your lifetime. That means no more going off the hinges when dinner is late. You must also learn to control your neurotic sense of internal lack. This card's other potential hazard would be getting bogged down in the day-to-day grind and routine. Don't be afraid to mix things up and try something new. The universe naturally encourages change. The more we can integrate change into our lives the happier the universe will be with us long-term. As much as we feel things are staying the same in our lives, I can assure you that the universe is perpetually in flux. Even mountains of stone get chiseled away by the sands of time!

Dates associated with this card

January 13th, February 12th, March 11th, April 10th, May 9th, June 8th, July 7th, August 6th, September 5th, October 4th, November 3rd, December 2nd.

> *For anything worth having one must pay the price; and the price is always work, patience, love, self-sacrifice - no paper currency, no promises to pay, but the gold of real service.*
>
> *John Burroughs*

5 of Cups

This is the dark side of the emotional sphere. Perhaps you were a Goth kid growing up, or had a morbid dark sense of life on earth.

Austin Muhs

Maybe you're just really into heavy metal, Tim Burton and black makeup. I jest, but this card isn't joking when it talks about finding a positive outlet for your emotional angst. Perhaps you would be happiest playing the blues, constantly living out your sorrows on stage. Maybe you want to be a tormented actress or perhaps you just enjoy unhealthy and painful relationships. My advice would be just to try and transmute all of this questionable emotional energy in a positive outlet of some kind. Art, relationship counseling, art therapy, musical decompression, all of which would apply to you! The positive thing is that no one kind of energy is inherently bad. You always will be given a chance to change your fate if you're willing to give just a bit of effort. Your happiness may lie in helping ease others' pain.

Negative

The card's dark side results in a perpetual breakup and a repeat type of lifestyle, where heartbreak becomes almost an addiction. I believe that life means you end up living out a bad repeat loop and enjoying it to one degree or another. It's somewhat odd but this is a card that needs a lot of emotional transformation work, letting go and deconstruction, to feel truly fulfilled. By alleviating emotional pain and old patterns, you are actually changing the world. "Be a leader, not a follower" should be your mantra!

Dates associated with this card

January 14th, February 13th, March 12th, April 11th, May 10th, June 9th, July 8th, August 7th, September 6th, October 5th, November 4th, December 3rd.

The Soul System of Tarot

The walls we build around us to keep sadness out but also keeps out the joy.

Jim Rohn

6 of Cups

This artistic card focuses on pleasure. You would excel at planning out new types of experiential businesses and art exhibits. You would make a brilliant promoter – as long as you believed in the harmonious nature of the work with which you were presenting. Working to construct sustainable dating systems or networks or matchmaking would be another natural choice for you. You may also be blessed with a knack for interior design or as a personal stylist. Creative planning is one of your strong suits and is a fuel for long-term passion. You could join the civic works planning commission, aiding in the planning of new parks and other beautification elements for your local city or town. Perhaps you just have a deep empathy for others. You would be excellent at personal care, or in-home care worker. You would derive personal satisfaction devoting free time to the elderly or the underprivileged. Anything that involves socialization with others is an intelligent route for you to take.

Negative

Beware of becoming a philanderer and becoming addicted to sensual vices. This can lead to a long trend of selfishness or narcissism if caution is not paid. You could also become something of an energy vampire if you're not careful. Remember a person only has as many masters as they have vices. The world's truly free people

Austin Muhs

are those truly dedicated to their own purification process: people actively working to transmute the shadow side into something meaningful and sustainable. If we are not continually clearing out karmic garbage and bad habits from our life then we risk the danger of becoming stuck in these denser energies.

Deep down we all want to do our best. We are all given the skills needed for success. However, it's a considerably more difficult task when you actually put all of your skills into practice in the real world. For most of you that takes effort. Even if we only have a few marketable skills at the outset, the fear of failure bred into us during childhood can paralyze us, making sustainable progress impossible. Beware of falling into all talk, no action cycles – this leads to cycles where nothing is achieved. All attempts at pumping your own ego only leads to a lack of respect from anyone. Stay humble! Let your actions speak for themselves! The surface level of life has many distractions, which keep you busy for as long as you let them. Don't get distracted on the surface of life: dig deep, and pull the meaning from the depths of your soul and work to realize your true potential for change.

Dates associated with this card

January 15th, February 14th, March 13th, April 12th, May 11th, June 10th, July 9th, August 8th, September 7th, October 6th, November 5th, December 4th.

I don't have a girlfriend. But I do know a woman who'd be mad at me for saying that.

Mitch Hedberg

The Soul System of Tarot

7 of Cups

This is one of the best cards for anyone with aspirations for being a writer; anyone with this card should give some thought with regard to his or her own personal and professional communications abilities. Perhaps you have never thought of using your creative gifts as a job. It's best that you not hide your unique mind underneath a rock. You are one of society's sci-fi type visionaries capable of leading people into a whole new future with cutting edge ideas and elongated verbal diatribes. You are the explorer of the subconscious. Perhaps you will find a home in subjects dealing with hollow earth, conspiracy, ufology or just outright outlandish fictional concepts. The key lies in utilizing the deep creativity sitting right in your noggin! If you fail to get in touch with your knowledge then you may find yourself perpetually stuck on life's surface level. Pursuing pleasure for it's own sake is a never-ending pursuit. Just be prepared to tread on un-trodden ground and take no holy-cows prisoner. You also have a deep capacity for changing the planet's unhealthy sexual patterns and transmuting them into something idiosyncratic and beautiful. Celibacy might be very helpful for you and your creative process: it would work to purify your thoughts, life and intentions. Remember you can become whom you truly want to be. It just requires a bit of effort!

Negative

This is a difficult card to keep motivated. Consistent with the seven archetypes there is an inherent self-sabotage motif present within this card. It may be difficult for you to find motivation. Emotional cycles may prevent long-term success. You may be looking at your career irrationally; heck you might be a flat out liar and manipulator. You also have your share of sexual quandaries and could be something of a psychic vampire until you learn to heal your dark side and channel more spiritual motives into your life. Dating is fraught with self-sabotage. Beware of any harm you cause others. With you, unhealthy patterns will eventually end up falling back upon your head. Refrain from drug usage. Also avoid any proclivities towards manipulation as well. Remember all base level sexual energy should be transmuted into martial arts, creative pursuits or anything that channels your energy into positive high-minded intellectually challenging activities. Whenever you become bored with life, sex becomes your go-to escapist activity – the key is to not to become bored. You can achieve this by adding structure to your life and not giving yourself enough free time to cause trouble. Idle hands are the devil's play things!

Dates associated with this card

January 16th, February 15th, March 14th, April 13th, May 12th, June 11th, July 10th, August 9th, September 8th, October 7th, November 6th, December 5th.

> *I think it is the height of ignorance to believe that the sexual act is an independent function necessary like sleeping or eating. Seeing, therefore, that I did not desire more children, I began to strive after self-control. There was endless difficulty in the task.*
>
> *Mahatma Gandhi*

The Soul System of Tarot

8 of Cups

This card teaches how and when to let go: it allows people to understand the difference between what's necessary and what's expendable. This is the supreme card of positive detachment. You might find a new ethos that helps redefine society's spiritual direction. Perhaps you will investigate the phenomenon of energy vampirism and how people fall victim to such traps. Perhaps you learn to identify society's unproductive methodologies and find ways to reform them by inventing systems designed to replace them. You can master the art of willingly taking life's more challenging path. You find the confidence to leave society's safety-sealed zones and reach out into the deeper (sometimes darker) corners of human existence. You could be a traveling wanderer or backpacker, always looking for your next spiritual quest. You might want to busy yourself with finding value out of what others regard as valueless. If you can find value in the seemingly useless world of the "inanimate", then you will truly be on a path towards meaningful self-discovery. Everything in the world has a life and deserves at least a modicum of our consideration. Respect others and the universe will in turn respect you. You only get what you give. Careers are found by helping those who are lost find their way. If you can help people to turn back to themselves and leave behind preconceived notions of what society has taught them to be, then you will have found your calling. Stopping to face your demons can be difficult but there always comes a day when you have to stop running and face what's chasing you.

Austin Muhs

Negative

If you are operating from this archetype's shadow you will be reluctant to really dig deep and understand your life's deeper issues. You might choose the safety sealed corporate community life – trying to play it safe in hopes of insulating your life from troubling emotions, but in the process also walling off any meaningful change. You could be lethargic when opportunity knocks, and let good things pass you by. You may feel as if the world will craft your destiny, but it is not the world's responsibility. A general sense of false superiority or snobby-ness can persist here. You need to maintain a humble, grounded and genuine nature. Running away from life and from yourself solves nothing. Avoidance is akin to fear and fear can control you if you let it. Remember, on the whole, life is meant to be a challenge. If this wasn't so than we would all be able to manifest things instantly in our life. Obviously we cannot acquire whatever we want instantaneously. Instead, we must fully exert ourselves to achieve our aims. Sometimes this even means throwing ourselves into seemingly uncomfortable or unsavory circumstances for the sake of personal growth. If you are just in it for yourself, others will notice and will not offer any genuine support of their own. If you are only looking out for number one, then you may never find your true place in this world.

Dates associated with this card

January 17th, February 16th, March 15th, April 16th, May 15th, June 14th, July 13th, August 12th, September 11th, October 10th, November 9th, December 8th.

The Soul System of Tarot

What is needed, rather than running away or controlling or suppressing or any other resistance, is understanding fear; that means, watch it, learn about it, come directly into contact with it. We are to learn about fear, not how to escape from it.

Jiddu Krishnamurti

9 of Cups

This is one of the most public and creative cards in the deck. It important to remember that with this card you should not fear the creative limelight. It is something to be embraced, not feared. You will be able to really make your mark in the world if you have the wherewithal to go it alone and dedicate yourself primarily to your creative talents. Otherwise you may find yourself at home in some fulfilling family unit scenario where you are able to get the reciprocal love and affection you crave through more traditional means. You should never have to give up on your creative dreams, much to the contrary. Embracing the arts of music, dancing, performance, drama and the public stage are major keys to your success. If you can embrace your inner artistic muse, you will put yourself high in the running for being a helpful considerate member of society.

Giving back to charitable endeavors is also key to your success. It's hard to really understand the long-term ramifications of your actions, but paying it forward will always work out supremely well for you. To obtain best results, be kind and generous with all those you meet. Perhaps you love to paint or do arts and crafts, whatever medium you can share with the rest of the world is where you should look to for universal support of your dreams.

The odd paradox within you is that you are happiest when other people are happy. Deep down you may fear that perpetual peace may never bless your life, which creates a paradox. Remember, if you bring happiness to others, you are healing yourself and opening up their goodwill towards you. You are creating the peace you crave one person at a time. Despite any fears, long-term you should have no problem finding a fulfilling life, as long as you are willing to dole out the effort.

Negative

On the downside of this archetype: when you finally make a buck, this archetype may cause you to blow through all your newfound cash reserves. If you are not careful, you can become an overindulgent hedonist. Remember, everything in moderation, or following the middle path is always the best option. The downfall here is trying to love too much or give too much. You need to understand when to stop and say no, healthy boundaries are a big deal for you. You can't throw yourself under the bus emotionally, fiscally or physically to spare others the pain of their karmic existence. This really equates to doing them a disservice as you are preventing them from the powerfully transformative psychological experience that comes along with just such pain.

Dates associated with this card

January 18th, February 17th, March 16th, April 15th, May 14th, June 13th, July 12th, August 11th, September 10th, November 9th, December 8th.

The Soul System of Tarot

The cardinal rule for any performer is that they should know themselves before they enter the spotlight, and I didn't. I was just Neil and I did what I was supposed to do. I was supposed to get married, so I got married. I was supposed to get a job, so I looked for work.

Neil Diamond

Ten of Cups

This is an archetype of family and love and togetherness. Whatever business you pursue, working with a spirit of personal achievement is a good plan. Perhaps you would like to be an announcer of some kind, or maybe you like to focus on personal growth for yourself or those around you. Obviously with this imagery in mind, a family type profession would suit you perfectly. Perhaps you would like to start a day care, or teach adult enrichment classes of one sort or another. Maybe you would like to make your living as a motivational speaker inspiring others. There really is no limit to the range of activities that this can encapsulate, it really just comes down to working in a spirit of harmony and emotional balance. Politics might also present a positive career option if you can work in a spirit of bringing harmony to the people.

Negative

You need to be on guard for being overly emotionally driven to the point of being logically irrational. Avoid being vague or indefinite in your communication with others. If mental health or mood swings are a concern, find appropriate natural remedies through acupuncture or alternative medicine. Regulating diet can also be helpful in this capacity as well. Compulsive drives can also haunt you if you are not the type to be naturally in tune with what you want out of life. This may take long- term mitigation strategies until you are able to balance yourself naturally and find that center point that you so fervently seek. Look to draw strength from cultural or community activities if you are looking for something to fortify you when you're feeling out of touch. Long-term happiness comes from within, so a need for an emotional outlet is a must for long-term emotional progression. I believe we are meant to do more than just feel emotions. We are meant to understand their deeper life purpose. If we really understand our emotional nature we can effectively couple that with the intellect and transmute otherwise impassable life barriers. Remember, emotions are akin to water, one of the strongest, versatile substances the world has known. It is able to penetrate virtually everything and with enough of it, great changes are exerted. As soft as water is it can generate enormous amounts of force. That force can then go on to create large scale sweeping change, almost as though a tidal wave had swept over the land. This is how true emotionality can be harnessed for massive societal change.

Dates associated with this card

January 19th, February 18th, March 17th, April 16th, May 15th, June 14th, July 13th, August 12th, September 11th, November 10th, December 9th.

> *The requirements for our evolution have changed. Survival is no longer sufficient. Our evolution now requires us to develop spiritually - to become emotionally*

The Soul System of Tarot

aware and make responsible choices. It requires us to align ourselves with the values of the soul - harmony, cooperation, sharing, and reverence for life.

Gary Zukav

Suit of Swords

The swords always deal with the mind and the intellect. Generally, they govern rational thought and different forms of technical or scientific expertise. Being methodically and logically driven can lead to an emotional sense of self being cut off. This can lead to personality issues, unless there is another active stabilizing or benevolent influence in the chart to counteract this energy. This type of archetype at its worst can lead to an atheistic, success at all costs mindset. I believe, in one form or another, we have all seen how this type of behavior works. This is a very common motif in movies amongst evil villains. They are geniuses but using their talents for the wrong reasons.

This archetype's positive side is a bit more encouraging: it is made up of famous musicians, scientists, computer programmers, engineers, and theologians. They also excel in areas such as divination, psychology and philosophy. The swords drive people to plumb the mind's deeper reservoirs in search of the truth behind themselves and their immediate reality. Being of the swords' family is great, but it also can be demanding; too much time can be spent running through your own mind. You can be highly intelligent, but too much intelligence can also come with a degree of depression if it is not rooted in some sense of spiritual purpose. Being intellectually superior to others doesn't mitigate any longstanding insecurity, as those on the archetype's lower octave will learn. Sometimes they are prone to white lies to help cover for their insecurities. Luckily this is a childish habit that many of them outgrow!

It's a strange thing that life ascribes different people, totally different theologies of how to go about finding a personal vocation. With the sword archetype as your driving factor, you might have that nagging feeling that if you can learn enough or if you can just absorb enough practical or spiritual knowledge, then you might be able to someday become enlightened or find some way to conquer the matter that seems to be oppressing you. When in actuality knowledge can become a hindrance at a certain point in spiritual development. In the Tao they have a saying: "Those who want to become smart learn something everyday, while those who want to become wise forget something everyday." This speaks to the counterintuitive nature of many supposed spiritual studies. Before you can learn, you must first de-clutter your mind

The difficult part is that when you are coming from a purely scientific world viewpoint, trying to understand that some of the best things in life cannot be logically explained can be difficult. This hearkens back to concepts I discussed in my first book Startup Fever, with regards to how "modern science" is claiming to be able to fix the world and solve all of the problems of human existence and spirituality, yet in the hundreds of years that we have been using science to "improve our lives", we are no closer to any spiritual answers about life than we were at the beginning of their creation. In fact we have really accomplished little; unless enslaving ourselves to the technology that was supposed to be empowering us can be called an accomplishment. Scientists tell us that "eventually," at some future point, they will have it all figured out. Creation will be

The Soul System of Tarot

reduced to some form of stoic life equation. I highly doubt any true spiritual renaissance will come from the people who brought us such things as the atomic bomb and Monsanto, just to name a few…

Now that is not to say that we toss aside logic and view everything as a perpetual indefinite in the universe, but it does say that logic alone has its limitations. In my view, first and foremost, we should all whole-heartedly pursue our spiritual studies on an individual level. These internal battles are the most important, most difficult battles we will ever face. This is why the Tarot is so important and effective for us: it will reveal our inner enemies (shadow self) who will oppose our spiritual quest and seek the self-destruction of our entire being. Those brave enough may be able to eventually overcome the shadow self, but I can wholeheartedly guarantee that everyone will have shadow problems during the beginning phases of their personal awakening process.

To me the swords are all about discovering reality's true nature. Usually the truth is a bitter pill that can be very hard to swallow. Human beings have a hard time accepting the quite obvious – we lack ultimate control over our life's entirety. If we had total control, none of us would willingly choose a path filled with as much suffering. I really feel it's necessary for us to understand that the more we can heal ourselves of society's negative programing and trappings, the more reality we will be able to handle, see and embrace. This quest truly encapsulates the highest motivations of those residing within the suit of the swords. The motto of the swords should be "Truth above all else". The swords may be mentally painful, as they force us to cut out parts of ourselves that we would rather stay intact. But it's better to let cancerous thoughts die than to engender them until they metastasize into a deadly spiritual parasite.

In the Tao Te Ching Lao Tzu states "The Tao that can be named is not the true Dao", effectively stating that words are cheap, and the transference of information via linguistics has its limitations. No matter what we choose to pursue with our lives, I believe what is most important is to engage the entirety of our being into it. If we leave our heart on the sidelines, fearing that it might become damaged if we show our passion to others, than we risk losing the ability to use our heart. Showing your true feelings might be painful, but once you are able to deeply accept yourself for who you are, then others will then be able to accept you as well.

Ace of Swords

This is actually the archetype of divination itself. It serves to bring clarity to all situations, separate people from their reckless passions, and bring a single-mindedness of purpose into your life. The sword has been used for thousands and thousands of years as a way to fight evil and help human beings define a sense of spiritual discipline and personal power within their lives. If you are not actively involved with fighting evil on some existential level, you may want to consider it. You possess a natural knack for fighting the darkness in your life with truth. Truth naturally scatters the evil in this world. The crazy part is that the truth doesn't even need to be spoken to retain power. In fact truth is best kept silent, as it's been my experience that the best teaching is done through action. People can learn through example and osmosis. It's a hard phenomenon to explain until you have seen it with your own eyes.

Evil is the bane of this dimension. Fighting evil on a personal one-to-one level is a way to accrue good fortune for ourselves in this life

The Soul System of Tarot

and beyond. Some people fight evil externally by helping and healing others. Others focus on purifying themselves and dispelling their inner shadows. However you prefer to accomplish such a feat, the important thing is to actually do the work. Time after time people fear to take the field of battle because they fear change or other repercussions for their actions. Fear should never be your guide – it will always bring a more difficult scenario than faith. When we doubt ourselves, we are selling ourselves short. That being said, I ask you to consider professions that allow you to help others conquer their own personal shadow side. In one way or another you can be doing a great service with the intellectual guidance and clarity that you bring to humanity.

You might also be a powerful force in discovering the forces behind the world's power structures that serve to enslave humanity. If you can break through these psychological boundaries within yourself, you can lead the way for others to do the same. Prepare yourself to face more than your fair share of moral quandaries with this archetype. This card will force you to use your spiritual compass time and again to sharpen your mental blade so to speak. You could become an expert researcher, a very prominent scientist, or anything that helps you gain logical and spiritual clarity. Uncovering the unknown and running in where others fear to tread are perfect vocational duties for you. Perhaps you want to become an astrologer, a Tarot reader, a marital artist, a psychologist, a philosopher, a researcher, a scientist, a healer, a fighter, a social rebel, a community reformer, a pioneer, an explorer or occupy any profession that forces you out of your comfort zone. This is an archetypal spiritual teacher card, allowing you to break out of the conventional 9-5 scenarios. Your discernment may make others uncomfortable but that's just part of your quest. You need to realize that being able to see through others will always make them uncomfortable on one level or another.

Negative

This archetype is quite capable of calculated cold-blooded evil. If this is your personal archetype, you must guard your morality with your life. You will be constantly seduced by the pleasures and inanities of the hedonistic world. You will be enticed to use your expert manipulative and deceptive abilities for the dark side. Perhaps you would want to become involved in organized crime, prostitution, murder, extortion, racketeering, embezzlement, fraud or the like. Obviously these choices would not end well for you. No true inner peace comes from illicit activities that serve to darken the human spirit. You will always be tempted. You have to be strong enough internally in order to resist the illusory momentary rewards of this life, understanding this world for the spiritual hologram that it is. You are meant to be a teacher; generally the best way to teach is to lead by example. Words are cheap, while actions can be priceless. Remember, no matter how secretive you think you are being, someone is always watching.

Dates associated with this card

January 20th, February 19th, March 18th, April 17th, May 16th, June 15th, July 14th, August 13th, September 12th, October 11th, November 10th, December 9th.

> *We can easily forgive a child who is afraid of the dark;*
> *the real tragedy of life is when men are afraid of the light.*
>
> *Plato*

The Soul System of Tarot

2 of Swords

Cooperation and teamwork are the name of the game for this archetype. Whatever you do, you should always try to incorporate like-minded individuals of spiritual merit to help you achieve your aims. Working together with a solid team creates an unstoppable force. "No man is an island" should be your motto. You have great ability to bring people together and mitigate conflict – it would be a crime not to put such talents to use. So remember, go forth and find your vocational brethren, moving forward with the spirit of friendship, companionship and human kinship in mind. Perhaps you will be drawn to the legal world since you naturally love to look at both sides of an issue. Perhaps you are interested in team building, historical revisionism, becoming a judge, being a homemaker (mitigating conflict in the household), a musician or an agent. Perhaps you will become proficient at some form of combat weaponry such as a two-pronged weapon of some kind. Perhaps you would enjoy working for others being a metallurgist or a composer. You could be an international diplomat or an interpreter. You should have a knack for anything that brings harmony through clear sightedness. Making decisions on the fly could end up being amongst your strong suits!

Negative

On the negative side, you could fall into the trap of creating discord wherever you go, operating from a selfish mentality such as: "If I can't be friends with them, than neither shall you". If you can work to transmute your shadow side and actively seek to facilitate harmony then you will become a valued asset in the community and amongst friends. This also pertains to marital partners, suppose you choose to marry someone who is naturally combative. The thing is that this weakness can eventually become the relationship's strength if you let it. You can find a path to peace within the relationship and then help guide others there once you learn the building blocks required for positive relationships. Or you could try (key word being try) to avoid this type of partner by looking at the person's true spiritual nature, their astrological/Tarot chart and their long-term intent for their own life. Looking past the superficial meanings and pleasure oriented escapes built into relationships will allow a clearer view of our own personal future. Obviously if you're really not sure about somebody you could always do a reading for yourself or seek the advice of a competent divination expert. You should learn as much as you can about that person via astrology and this Soul System Divination method – this will give you supreme insight into that persons subconscious motives and weaknesses. Love is always a tricky thing, especially when you are signing a contract that binds you to another person for a lifetime…for these types of decisions, a sober, wise and competent third party analysis is always advised. Occasionally everyone needs a devil's advocate to show us a viewpoint outside the rose colored glasses of love.

Dates associated with this card

January 21st, February 20th, March 19th, April 18th, May 17th, June 16th, July 15th, August 14th, September 13th, October 12th, November 11th, December 10th.

> *Non-cooperation with evil is as much a duty as is cooperation with good.*
>
> *Mahatma Gandhi*

The Soul System of Tarot

3 of Swords

When I see the three of swords I always think of the emotional last blow of a relationship – its not always needed, but it always seems to happen. Just when you think you are safe and have ended something amicably, there comes the other party trying to get your goat one last time. Obviously this is never a fun situation. The good news: with this as your archetype you are able to channel these emotionally disquieting energies into a much grander intellectual vision. Perhaps you are a playwright specializing in writing neo-tragedies, or perhaps you are someone who likes to deconstruct decrepit structures in society.

With this as your archetype I would look at destruction as a way to make money. Look at careers in demolitions, liquidations, finding ways to terminate useless positions in corporate America, business consulting, family law attorneys, community reform, advocates for the less fortunate or forgotten, volunteer worker, firefighter, ER doctor, trauma specialist, burn specialist, reconstructive surgeon. You can make a big impact helping others make it through difficult psychological times. Any profession that allows you to speak your true thoughts, while helping others in dire emotional circumstances should help you find fulfillment. You need to work out the distress accrued from past lives in order to truly be happy in this one. You need to let the emotionality pass through you. Don't hang on to it, hoping it will go away on its own. Perhaps you find a home amongst rehabilitation programs of one form or another. You find faith in the most unlikely places and pull yourself out of this world's delusions. One could say that this world is a series of traps: no one will come to understand this concept better than you!

Austin Muhs

Negative

The negative side: if you don't find an outlet for this archetype's negative emotional energies than expect negativity in your life. Emotional transmutation through creativity or spiritual service is crucial to your evolvement. You could be someone struggling with ongoing depression, bi-Polar disorders, emotional self-sabotage, negative entities, addictions, emotional irrationality, negative experiences in love relationships, a damaged view of your own self worth, struggling to make new friends, feeling isolated or dejected. You could be subjected to a whole cocktail of mental instability in various forms. Don't let the destructive archetype rain over your own life, use it to your advantage! Drug addiction and living in the pain of the past are also to be avoided!

Dates associated with this card

January 22nd, February 21st, March 20th, April 19th, May 18th, June 17th, July 16th, August 15th, September 14th, October 13th, November 12th, December 11th.

> *History, despite its wrenching pain, cannot be unlived, but if faced with courage, need not be lived again.*
>
> *Maya Angelou*

4 of Swords

This archetype best typifies someone who would make a great doctor or healer. Believe it or not you may also be a natural for being a detective. This archetype promises great potential, but also promises hard mental labors of some kind. Doctors are always searching for cures, researchers are always searching for answers, and paleontologists are always digging for clues. Reading and research should always be pursued – if you don't use your mind, you will lose your mind. That's right, you are the type that will be susceptible to Alzheimer's or other debilitating mental conditions because if you are not using your mind your spirit will get bored and check out early. Always remember to utilize your mental prowess to its fullest. You have a life purpose – embrace it and be passionate about your interests. Write books about things that you know and love. Make new discoveries and teach the less fortunate when you have free time. The key is to always stay mentally flexible and vibrant.

One of my astrology teachers was influenced by this archetype; it forced her to look to astrology to learn why her life ended up the way that it did. Anything that forces you to peacefully quest for life's underlying meaning should work well for you. This is also a great archetype for someone looking to become a teacher or professor. It allows you to integrate vast troves of data in an entertaining way. You will not always have time to pursue your said objectives so you need to heed the day. This sign always searches for truth and always able to see beneath the surface. Many of this sign have psychic gifts, albeit many times in a latent state.

Negative

Avoid secret societies with this card. The power afforded by them is illusory and meaningless to individualistic advancement. If they offered society any harmonious answers then we wouldn't be living in a perpetual war zone on the other side of the globe. Instead these groups will prey on your so-called negative motives and try to convince you of their benevolent ideologies. Here's a news flash, collectivism in any form is rarely a benevolent enterprise. No one can offer you supreme enlightenment other than yourself. Anything of spiritual merit in this world will require total dedication to achieve – something these small time, petty, power brokers know very little about. Their knowledge is limited – they only know how to build a structure that lands them at the top of the heap. Those who are serious about spiritual studies and advancement usually fly solo when possible: they realize the dangers unhealthy collectives pose to their own intuitive course of action.

You always want to be cognizant of your physical health. Hidden ailments might plague you at crucial times. Some of these influences can be mitigated through doing good karmic works. If you are working within established structures such as academia, you need to be careful not to tow the party line. This is akin to selling your soul for a safe job, instead of teaching deep truths uncovered in your studies. This is also a key concept for you to embody as well!

Dates associated with this card

January 23rd, February 22nd, March 21st, April 20th, May 19th, June 18th, July 17th, August 16th, September 15th, October 14th, November 13th. December 12th.

> *I think the job of leadership is to expand what can be talked about and to get consensus on the nature of the problem, and that is most of the job. Because once you do that, once you have diagnosis, treatment options are obvious.*
>
> *Jim Cooper*

The Soul System of Tarot

5 of Swords

This is an archetype that allows you to mitigate and avoid conflict. Time itself will be your greatest teacher while, over the years, you figure out bigger and better ways to harmonize working methods. You would benefit by integrating meditation or some other quiet activity into your morning ritual routine. Through the silence you will find your clear subconscious answers and the true source of your wisdom. Overthinking things offers no help, it will only drive you further within yourself during your quest for answers. Look to careers where you specialize in problem solving and conflict resolution. It seems as though not dealing with work stress might not be an option for your archetype, but dealing with the stress effectively and in a harmonious manner is always possible. Perhaps you would enjoy starting a naturalistic rehabilitation center for those with debilitating mental conditions or addictions. Or you might find yourself within the realms of business plan writing or developing new forms of organizational planning. Life coaching might be another excellent path for you. If you can first conquer the chaotic stressors of modern life, you can then go on to impart these methodologies to others. Life itself seems to reach out to you from time to time, making an effort to help you find yourself amidst the modern world's chaos – always heed that call. Spiritually speaking inaction is just as important as action. Often, we can accomplish more by cleaning our own internal world (which on the surface appears to be doing nothing) than by trying to fix the external world. As pointed out in the following quote by Lao Tzu: "The world is won by those who let go, but for those who try and try the world is beyond winning". This is sound advice for those driven to fill life with compulsive activities.

Negative

If you are not careful, this card can turn you into a downright worrywart. You may never feel able to really relax. Remember, everything happens in its due time. There is no need to wrestle your destiny to the ground. Instead, give it your best effort and know when to stop. Life is a wild, crazy ride, so prepare for the long haul. Never actively seek to exploit others: avoid envy, be honest, maintain cultural norms where needed, avoid the tendency to argue, and pick your partners wisely. Parts of your life will be spent picking up the pieces, but once you learn your lessons, (probably after your Saturn return at 30) then you will be well equipped to handle any chaotic form that life throws at you.

The wrong road would be believing that your life will always be difficult and then attempt to cheat life in one way or another. Remember, anything worth having takes time. Individual karma is a knotty subject to try and fully understand, so be patient. Always know that your time will come if your heart is in the right place. Life never really ignores our dreams, we just lose our commitment to the sustained effort it takes to achieve them. With enough patience anything is possible.

Dates associated with this card

January 24th, February 23rd, March 22nd, April 21st, May 20th, June 19th, July 18th, August 17th, September 16th, October 15th, November 14th, December 13th.

The Soul System of Tarot

In times of great stress or adversity, it's always best to keep busy, to plow your anger and your energy into something positive.

Lee Iacocca

6 of Swords

This is an amazing card for anyone looking to pursue a career in the musical arts, especially those looking to play an instrument or become a flutier. It's also a great card for those looking to get into the computer industry, the humanities, sciences, or just becoming a specialist in your particular field of choice. You should be a great researcher. You should seek advanced education or self-study. You thrive in all forms of communication. Networking and the like is a natural choice for you to gain professional advancement. You could also enjoy becoming a trainer in your professional field. You could become a detective, inventor, or anything that challenges you to look beneath reality's surface. The whole tech craze should hold much allure for you. In fact it was actually Steve Job's archetypal card. So all of you wannabe tech gurus out there, knock yourselves out. Anything that works to bring people together via communication should be a natural go to for you.

Negative

Beware of being cold, indifferent, calculating, selfish, self-possessed, intellectually arrogant and the like. When taken to an extreme any of these traits can bring a multitude of problems. You must realize that just because you may be smarter than others it doesn't guarantee that you are morally or spiritually superior. It's time to drive home the fact that there is always someone that will be better than you and there is always more to learn in life. Remaining humble is the best option no matter what future great things you might achieve. That will keep you safe from those who like to cast stones and cast them in your general vicinity.

Staying true to your roots is key for you. You should understand that in order for you to have an elevated position, someone else must be put below. This is how to stay humble because as in some other lifetime it is pretty much guaranteed that you have occupied a lowly position somewhere along the way. These are key elements, enabling you to maintain your spiritual self during any successes you may encounter vocationally. Obviously Steve Jobs was also a vicious boss, destroying people with his words. He cultivated an aura of fear, which, in my opinion, is something to be avoided. Try your best to cultivate a deeply meaningful leadership style. You can maintain your integrity and avoid cultivating enemies.

Dates associated with this card

January 25th, February 24th, March 23rd, April 22nd, May 21st, June 20th, August 19th, September 18th, November 17th, December 16th

The single biggest problem in communication is the illusion that it has taken place.

George Bernard Shaw

The Soul System of Tarot

7 of Swords

This is a really a diverse card to have, on one level it makes you into a true individual who in order to create their path is almost forced outside of the norm. On another level it really makes things more difficult as you can make things overly complex. For best success you need to choose a profession that is far from the mainstream. Perhaps you would enjoy being a travelling performer, a reformist monk, a dream analyst, a hostage negotiator, or an aerial rescue expert. Whatever you find yourself doing, crafting seemingly impossible solutions is something you thrive at. Perhaps you want to be the next Nikola Tesla, or a trend setting fashion mogul like Salvador Dali was. Again the options are only limited by your imagination and the need to use your complex and genius mind for a good cause. Tense negotiation types of work also work well for you, as you are able to utilize your craftier personality traits in a productive way.

Negative

Being a very complex character it might be easy for you to fall victim to this card's dark side. Someone operating on this card's dark side may lean towards being a sociopath and/or narcissist who is willing to lie to get whatever it is that they currently desire. However you look at it there will be a need for deep emotional healing work for true long-term success in your vocational life. This does not mean that you will not be successful, quite the contrary. It's just that success not rightfully earned, is never long lasting. Above all you need to focus on developing a solid sense of purpose, integrity and make a habit of sticking to your word. If you don't have your word in this world, then you don't have much! You should also beware of not fully committing, keeping secret agendas, or being overly impractical. When you are able to avoid manipulation and escapism in all of its permutations, it will mean you have hit a pivotal point in your spiritual development. Remember that life has it's own way of helping things to work out in the end. It's not up to us to micro-manage or manipulate our own lives.

Dates associated with this card

January 26th, February 25th, March 24th, April 23rd, May 22nd, June 21st, July 20th, August 19th, September 18th, October 17th, November 18th, December 17th.

> *In the last few years, the very idea of telling the truth, the whole truth, and nothing but the truth is dredged up only as a final resort when the alternative options of deception, threat and bribery have all been exhausted.*
>
> *Michael Musto*

8 of Swords

This type can be a born psychologist. It's best if you delve deeply into things so that you are really able to make the most out of these talents. Perhaps you can work to help heal those with addiction issues or discover injustices out in the world. Also high on my list for you would actually be exorcist or paranormal investigator. Now that may seem crazy, but dealing with things that go bump in the night might just be a hidden talent of yours. Its hard to say exactly

The Soul System of Tarot

in what form or function you will find your true calling doing such work but I can say that you might have a natural knack for it if you gave it a shot! Now am I not telling you to go off and join the Vatican's ranks (not the case), but perhaps understanding the demon world phenomenon (which is more impactful than anyone wants to admit) might be worth your while. Searching for and dishing out punishments to the world's evils is a vocational knack you have, but this quest to right wrong starts from within. Also dealing with dream work or those incarcerated might be a good line of work for you. People in prison are generally pretty destitute – perhaps you have the unique consciousness and constitution that will help them develop spiritual skills to escape their sense of karmic suffering.

Perhaps you want to work as a detective breaking up crime syndicates or perhaps you are a freedom fighter for political prisoners. Maybe you want to make your living as a journalist exposing human rights abuses. There are many different possibilities for you to find a meaningful vocation but it should always revolve around finding ways to heal the self-imposed slaveries, so prevalent within the human condition.

Negative

This card has a real dangerous dark side which incorporates such problems as addiction, lack of a conscience, being raised in a dangerous or immoral household, lacking faith in your own innate abilities, being afraid to be yourself, maintaining a pessimistic attitude, becoming a tyrant, or a liar. Whatever the case when you are working on this archetype's dark side you might be acting out the delinquency from your childhood. However you look at it, you need to find the source of your pain or spiritual struggle and work to heal it at the source. Acting out your aggressions or problems in the external world just serves to repeat the karmic cycle and will never allow you to fully escape your fate. Remember, there are darker dimensions that one can go to if you are totally immoral in this one. Even if you have started down a dark path in your early days, there is always time to turn back. You need to look deep within yourself to realize that by healing yourself, you heal the rest of the world. You then can begin to assist those people who suffer from similar problems, or who have suffered at the hands of a similar fate.

Dates associated with this card

January 27th, February 26th, March 25th, April 24th, May 23rd, June 22nd, July 21st, August 20th, September 19th, November 18th, December 17th.

Destroy the seed of evil, or it will grow up to your ruin.

Aesop

9 of Swords

I like to think of this as a Joan of Arc archetype, where you wake up one day and just see through the hollowness of the world and are then able to craft your destiny by the guiding light of your inner self. You could find solace working with others who suffer from depression, existential purposelessness, grief or the like. As mental agony is no stranger to you, you are in turn well equipped to deal with the drama and disturbance within other people's lives. Time is your greatest friend if you let it be. Perhaps you are interested in writing spiritual or psychological works to help others find themselves. Perhaps you are interested in writing about post apocalyptic works of science fiction, just don't drink your own Kool-Aid! There is always hope for the world, as this dimension is very fluid and changeable. Once you conquer your own worst-case scenario or self-masochistic forms of thinking, you can then go about helping others to do the same. Any dimension as fluid as earth always has hope. I would imagine that the many dimensions of hell are much more dense and harder to change due to the spiritual structure of their composition.

Negative

On this sign's dark side you can be plagued with nightmares, possession, bad health or a Debbie downer, pessimistic, doom and gloom, outlook. Lets turn that frown upside down there, mate! Looking on the bright side or being more optimistic in general could help the more forlorn brooders of this archetype. It becomes a matter of finding whatever motivating spiritual theology will help get you through the day. Keeping a good grasp on health matters should help you maintain a vigilant sense of clarity and purpose in your spiritual/emotional life. Practicing martial arts or other games of high strategy such as GO and chess would be helpful as well. This forces you to sharpen your mind along with your wit. Bad astrological cycles generally last 2.5 years, so if you find yourself on the receiving end of some life turmoil, just remember, it will change eventually. Nothing stays the same forever and the universe cannot entertain a void. Just take your own life with a degree of seriousness and dedication to higher ideals and you should be fine. Seek out

Austin Muhs

qualified healers within your preferred modality. I personally have a profound aversion to most western medicine unless you have been in a car wreck or you need a finger sown back on, but take your healing as you like it!

Dates associated with this card

January 28th, February 27th, March 26th, April 25th, May 24th, June 23rd, July 22nd, August 21st, September 20th, October 19th, November 18th, December 17th.

> *Quite a lot of our contemporary culture is actually shot through with a resentment of limits and the passage of time, anger at what we can't do, fear or even disgust at growing old.*
>
> *Rowan Williams*

10 of Swords

This is a card of total and complete commitment to the truth. It allows you to break through old paradigms in life and embrace the truth no matter what the cost. Perhaps you would like to make your living as a shock artist of some kind, projecting renegade movies onto buildings or rooftops. Maybe you would like to make your living studying conspiracies of one brand or another, taking time out to analyze and evaluate the long term viability of your plans is a major key with this card. Don't be shy to scrap rough drafts of your dreams and start again! You may have to try your hand at a few different things before finding success in your later days, but remember that peaking too late is much better than peaking too early. Facing small life failures will lead you to your big successes later on, if you let it! Find professions that allow you to get past the mundane and discard the unneeded. Perhaps you can reform the recycling industry. Maybe you find that dealing with grief counseling around death is transformative for you. You might also work well moonlighting with some form of voluminous literary work; something encyclopedic would be perfect. Look for a type of reference work that takes years to compile but will last beyond your lifetime. Perhaps you're at home creating an OCD catalog of some kind. Over the long term, these *Materia Medica* type documents can be more impactful than you may first realize. In many instances, these are also good karmic spiritual works. Helping others in the future to further their spiritual studies on the planet is always a good thing!

Negative

Avoid the temptation to become materialistic and attracting materialistic people into your life. Avoiding self-sabotage is the name of the game for you. You have a tendency to attract situations and people that serve to waste your time and energy. Perhaps you cannot view yourself as successful in the long run, or perhaps it just seems like an impossible task to achieve your dreams. Whatever the case I can assure you that all hope is not lost, you just have to dig deep and make it happen. I would avoid dealing with any morally questionable characters of any type unless you are supremely sure you can hold your own in the situation. I would also suggest avoiding any work with the disabled or the mentally deranged as you might be prone to absorbing chi from people with these conditions. If you don't believe me, go and take a look at most of the people who work in these particular trades. Younger clients that I have worked with have become severely drained by the work. In my experience one has to be a high level healer to be able to deal with these many times unsavory environments.

Dates associated with this card

January 29th, February 28th, March 27th, April 26th, May 25th, June 24th, July 23rd, August 22nd, September 21st, October 20th, November 19th, December 18th.

> *I'm for truth, no matter who tells it. I'm for justice, no matter who it's for or against.*
>
> Malcolm X

Suit of Disks

The disks, also known as pentacles, are the slowest moving of all of the card groups, but rest assured that when the disks do start move, the ground shakes. It's akin to the earth elements in astrology: aka Taurus, Capricorn, Virgo. Without the suit of disks archetypes many of the world's greatest monuments would never have been built because people of other suits might have become bored mid stream and given up. The disks types are in it for the long haul. They want to slowly and steadily reform society and meld it into putty in their hands. Even thought the disks' vocational foundations are mostly built upon material success and worldly achievement, it actually incorporates much more than just that. Generally speaking, the disks want to build for the sake of a better world – it just so happens that the disks are also going to value security first within their personal lives. This is where disagreements amongst family, friends, and colleagues may appear simply because other people don't really view security as some kind of Archimedean point that allows them to enjoy their life. Others see security as an existential albatross, or a weight on their shoulders from a past life of which they don't want to bear. I myself fall into the later category, as even though I like the freedom that money brings, I also understand the vast amount of responsibility that it carries in tow as well. There is really nothing free in this world.

As an example, let's analyze a rich businessman's life. He dies of a stress induced heart attack at the age of 50. How much better is that man's life than a middle class worker who lives to be 85? I would personally much rather have an additional 35 years to live, but I guess that's just a matter of perspective. I'm just pointing out that quality of life is what you are looking for, not living to excess – which is so common in the western world it is almost a paradigm for behavior. Excess has always been in fashion: it usually does little but attempt to cover up a person's deeper insecurities. Grandiosity is a product of the ego, as from my experience the true self much prefers meaningful growth in smaller gestures as opposed to big displays. Big displays always move a lot of energy and when you move a lot of energy there comes a risk that something can go awry. The main teaching of the disks is the old "slow and steady wins the race". For the suit of the disks, vocations are all about preparation and planning. They don't pretend to know what they don't know. Instead they will thoroughly study a topic and come back to you with a well-researched answer. These are the types of people that you would like to handle your money and to hold long-term planning decisions with. Now conversely, the lesser of the disks archetype would try to cheat the system or look for shortcuts. This is how you end up with corrupt government, as certain individuals are very patient when they are figuring out how to game the system and make very long term plans, which include corruption.

Ace of Disks

This is a very dynamic and entrepreneurial card. Perhaps you find yourself most at home in terms of material achievement or entrepreneurial success. I wouldn't say you should chase after money though for its own sake, instead focus on challenging yourself to produce useful goods and services for others in society. You will probably feel right at home in this age of crowdfunding which encourages entrepreneurship by helping people raise funds through group efforts. Services like this include websites such as Kickstarter and IndieGogo etc. If you are looking to start up a small business I would also recommend you check out my other book *Startup Fever, How crowdfunding Will Rebuild the American Dream* for additional tips on sustainable entrepreneurship. Or you could pretty much read any work the Ayn Rand ever wrote: I believe she is still the undisputed champion of moralistic grassroots economics.

Remember that in terms of economics, slow and steady wins the race. Whenever you are dealing with the suit of disks you are dealing with a slower moving energy, so proper preparation is a big key to your long-term success. This archetype can put you through large swings in material fortune, as with any risk takers there is always the downside of any professional venture. If this is your archetype, the key is to work on securing your stability internally, instead of externally. Time will judge whether you have built solid foundations

The Soul System of Tarot

in your mind, or if you were building castles in the sand. Whether we know it or not, reality is changing every second or every day and if we try to build a house in the shade of a tree, eventually the sunlight will creep in to show us what we had been missing while captured in the darkness.

In terms of career options you could become a small business owner, a venture capitalist, a stockbroker, an inventor, a pioneer, an investment advisor, a real estate agent, a grant writer, a biographer, a professor, a business mogul, etc. You would be good at any vocation that forces you to work to build yourself stability from the ground up. That being said, this archetype also has many fiscal ups and downs so learning to ride that roller coaster will help you long term. Remember no matter the external environment, you can always learn to balance yourself internally with spiritual fortitude and faith.

Negative

The downside of this archetype can be the money before all else mentality. Perhaps this has left you with a bitter sense of atheism and a feeling that you can actually control everything in our reality. Time will eventually show you that you cannot control everything, no matter how much success or material dominion you are able to muster. Again I will quote Lao Tzu, "The world is won by those who let go, for those who try and try the world is beyond winning". Don't be fickle with your affections or relationships will cost you much capital as well. You have an archetype that likes to choose superficial relationships with attractive partners who also happen to value superficial things more than the deep meaningful interactions. That means when you split it's a free-for-all battle-royale for the attorneys.

Austin Muhs

Just like any successful businessperson, you may be stuck learning your economic lessons the hard way, especially if your parents were in a poverty consciousness mindset. If that's the case then you will really need to work on deconstructing your subconscious patterns so you can heal them and move on. Doing good karmic works and being 100 percent ethical in all of your dealings will help to expedite this process. Not saying that everything you do will be perfect, but you need to go in with the motto that a project isn't really successful unless it's a win for your clients, yourself and society at large. Business is often a very unscrupulous place, so you will need to stick your neck out when appropriate to stand up for what's right. Pick your battles wisely and always be prepared for war if need be.

Dates associated with this card

January 30th, February 29th, (where applicable) March 28th, April 27th, May 26th, June 25th, July 24th, August 23rd, September 22nd, October 21st, November 20th, December 19th.

> *Money cannot buy peace of mind. It cannot heal ruptured relationships, or build meaning into a life that has none.*
>
> Richard M. DeVos

2 of Disks

This would be a great placement for someone who wanted to be a professional fundraiser for charitable endeavors of one kind or another. You have a real knack for getting people excited about your out-of-the-box projects and other ventures. Perhaps you enjoy being part of a financial co-op of some sort, (just beware of dependency sneaking in) making your living working together with others towards a greater good for society. You could embrace a jack-of-all-trades mentality while learning many different professions. You will then be able to freelance so you are in complete control of your own time table and vocational destiny. The good thing is that getting financing in general should be a strong suit of yours. Perhaps this lands you in the realm of real estate where you are constantly dealing with banks, escrow and the like. Or perhaps you are helping people to raise seed capital for their own businesses through crowdfunding or through angel investor pools. However you look at it, this should be one of the most exciting decades of your life with all of the new growth in these fundraising method arenas!

This card also lends itself to a jack-of-all trades mentality and allows you to comfortably freelance without too much concern about the long-term fiscal outlook. The key here is to let go of the notion that you have to build fiscal security, when in fact the security will build itself as long as you are applying all of your spiritual talents. When we try to force a vocation or a career path based on economics, the result is the sacrifice of our own soul's purpose. If we are to make our purpose walk the plank, so to speak, then there better be a darn good reason, or at least a reason better than just having security for security's sake. Nothing in this world is totally secure – trying to build up walls around you usually does as much to trap you in, as it does to keep others out. Vocations break down walls while quests for security can build them.

Austin Muhs

Negative

On the downside this card really represents someone who doesn't have much fiscal stability to speak of for most of his or her life. Perhaps chronic money mismanagement plagues them along with an expensive or extravagant lifestyle. However it happens, you may need to work on embracing the flow of money coming and going in waves instead of primarily focusing on accruing it. That might be a touchy play for you. In Feng Shui theory, money is akin to water, so try to remember that grasping a bucketful of water between your fingers is a fool's task, since when you try and grab too much, the water will always evade your grasp. Meditating upon this correlation between money and water for a minute will help you to understand the deeper meanings of finances, along with what it can or cannot do in your life. Water can sustain you, but if you drink too much you can die as well. At its root level, money is just stored energy, so having a healthy respect for the stored energy inherent within our lives will go a long ways towards a thriving economic disposition long-term. Again become comfortable with the flow of money in and out and there will be no problems. Fluctuation is the nature of your essence so why fight against it?

Dates associated with this card

January 31st, March 29th, April 28th, May 27th, June 26th, July 25th, August 24th, September 23rd, October 22nd, November 21st, December 20th.

> *Ironically, Latin American countries, in their instability, give writers and intellectuals the hope that they are needed.*
>
> *Manuel Puig*

The Soul System of Tarot

3 of Disks

This is a very artistic type of card compared to the other disks as it truly represents compiling a solid body of artistic work in one form or another. Time will fly for those who are passionately consumed within the depth of this vocational track. You can work virtually round the clock and probably thrive off deadlines whether you consciously like to admit it or not. This is not a card for the couch potato. This shows you being the most fulfilled in life when you are on the front lines out there making your passion visible for the rest of the world. Architecture, sculpting, painting, drafting schematics, museum curating, design work, fashion design, or anything involving a high level of trade craftsmanship should leave you happy and fulfilled by and large. There's no need for you to second guess your passion here. As time moves on you will generally try your hand at a number of these design mediums until you reach your peak later in life. This is a put up or shut up card, where you let your work speak for itself. If you don't create anything meaningful with your time, then you probably won't have a great career when you are dealing with this archetype.

This also gives you the ability to instruct as well, perhaps taking on a mentorship role later on down the line, bringing back the middle age apprenticeship mediums in one way or another. You can really show the world how to appreciate a job well done, because you know that doing your best when you're working on a project is a reward within itself.

Negative

If you are operating on the lower octave of this card then many of the typical starving artist's motifs may apply. You might have a hard time getting off the couch to make it happen for yourself. You might have to roll on faith from time to time to get you through. The bottom line being, if you are really fully applying yourself, you are never going to starve, you just have to stay active and stay hungry (no pun intended)! It may take you some time to find your true creative voice. Heck some artists die before people really start to appreciate their work. The important part is that they went out and created the work anyway. These "ahead of their time" artists understood that the vibration of the works that they were creating would have a positive long lasting psychological impact upon future generations. If it weren't for these people doing what they loved for its own sake, then the world would be in an even more barbarous state than we find it today, in my estimation. The work wasn't hard for them in an existential sense, it was their life's calling and so it amounted to the only viable option in their mind. If you are passionate and have a vision, then your life can be driven by something beyond superficial monetary pursuits.

One fact remains certain: the work will not do itself. When in doubt, try, try and try again. There is nothing like practice to make perfect as they say. I can assure you for those with a solid work ethic there is a light at the end of the tunnel and that light isn't a train! You might be forced into menial jobs or things that don't utilize all of your considerable talents, but suck it up! Nikola Tesla, undoubtedly the greatest inventor who has ever lived, single handedly compiling over 750 US patents, started his career in America by digging ditches. After that he had to work for his arch nemesis and professional idea-less hack and intellectual property thief, better known as Thomas Edison! Remember what Nikola said, as it my very well apply to your vocation dreams, "The present

The Soul System of Tarot

is theirs, but the future, for which I have really worked is mine"! Some may say this is an ego freak statement, but I'll be darned if he wasn't one hundred percent correct. As our entire technological infrastructure runs on his theories he had to have been a space alien!

Another key for you here is not to sell out. Never lower your standards and become a tool for corporate America. Remember you can't change the world by helping to build up the unhealthy and aberrant systems that are all around us. Maintain your ethical and moral standards at all costs or suffer the consequences!

Dates associated with this card

March 30th, April 29th, June 28th, July 27th, August 26th, September 25th, October 24th, November 23rd, December 22nd.

> *Opportunities are usually disguised as hard work, so most people don't recognize them.*
>
> *Ann Landers*

4 of Disks

One could think of this as an archetypal banker card. This card really allows people to save and secure money over the long term. This is a card of real estate managers, real estate developers, landowners, business magnates, accountants, corporate managers and executives and overall very patient people. The 4 of disks moves slowly so that nothing can disturb its long-term plans and far reaching economic visions. Perhaps you would be a wise economic counselor, or could help with raising funds for philanthropic causes like building temples, which can help others to find their own unique spiritual path. Temples can help mankind to find different kinds of salvation, healing, and existential advancement. Raising money for sustainable causes and donating land to creative and spiritual restorative enterprises are good routes to look at to fulfill your vocational destiny.

Negative

The downside here is becoming the Uncle Scrooge or uber materialist. You don't want to make your living at the expense of being a miser. Your legacy will be marred with jealousy hatred and anger. Without these things, it will be hard to understand what's really happening. This can find you also stuck strictly in the material world with no real regards for spirituality and its affects upon your life. It's always good to consider the longer-term spiritual consequences of all of your actions on your soul's legacy. Every action has a reaction, so working strictly in the material realm can hurt your longer-term spiritual progress as it takes up time you could have spent working on your internal self. So as a result, try and find a profession that merges your higher spiritual goals with a secure lifestyle. Number four cards always bring a degree of challenge so it may take you a while to achieve security but once it's in place, it should be there to stay!

Dates associated with this card

March 31st, April 30th, May 29th, June 28th, July 27th, August 26th, September 25th, October 24th, November 23rd, December 22nd.

> *Human progress is neither automatic nor inevitable...*
> *Every step toward the goal of justice requires sacrifice,*

The Soul System of Tarot

suffering, and struggle; the tireless exertions and passionate concern of dedicated individuals.

Martin Luther King, Jr.

5 of Disks

This is a great card for working with the needy or underprivileged. The main objective here is to frame your financial life in a meaningful way, superseding the preconceived notions of what money and wealth is supposed to mean in life. If you are able to reinvent your definition of money, then you are well on your way to achieving your new dream vocation. Things are always more difficult than we think them to be at the outset, so with the 5 of disks you need to work on maintaining an optimistic attitude no matter what circumstances were for you growing up or first starting out. It is usually the people who have overcome great hardships that become the most meaningful vocationalists long-term. Your struggle is your gift as I stated earlier in the book. Vocations take time to develop, so be patient with yourself. You would do well to start a non-profit or help those looking to reform their outlook on finance. This could incorporate life coaching and simple accounting and base level fiscal management on the lower level.

Again, work on restructuring economics into a more meaningful framework in the outside world is a natural occupational choice for you. It's all about embracing empathy and working to heal the inner poverty consciousness that so much of society has embraced during this time in human history. People need to understand that there is always enough to go around if you are working towards improving your karmic standing in the world. If you are committing evils out in the world, of course poverty can result, but that's just an end effect of your root cause actions. Areas of crowdfunding and sites such as GoFundMe represent good examples for you to model your plans after. The ideals represented in those companies are universal in their service and dedication toward others.

Negative

Being that this is the spiritual poverty card in a sense, on the downside you can feel a bit worthless. Perhaps you were born into a family during challenging financial times or perhaps they just did not do much to respect your sovereignty as a vocationally aspiring little youngster. Or maybe you just have a bitter taste left in your mouth from people around you who make money so easily (I know I did). Whatever the case may be you need to realize that your own monetary destiny is something you have to carve out for yourself. You have to let all the past stuff go. Fact is, the world is full of a lot of unsavory creatures and you will have to deal with many of them in working your way up the vocational ladder. Money isn't all there is to life, perhaps you have been blessed with a great personality, a loving significant other or a few true friends. Remember to be grateful for whatever you have been given, as in my experience there will always be people who are both more and less fortunate than you are. As meager as you feel your fortune may be, trust me its better than nothing. I mean, heck, you can read obviously, that's a leg up on what most people had 200 years ago. I have studied the cruel insanities that this world has to offer and trust me: you should be planning a spiritual exit plan. Whatever karma we face on earth, we just have to deal with it and move on. Taking spiritual responsibility for your own financial future and letting go of any entitlement attitudes will help you feel better about the situation. Find jobs that give you spiritual solace while allowing you to reform your existential viewpoints regarding personal wealth.

Dates associated with this card

May 30th, June 29th, July 28th, August 27th, September 26th, October 25th, November 24th, December 23rd.

> *A man who dares to waste one hour of time has not discovered the value of life.*
>
> Charles Darwin

6 of Disks

It's a beautiful day if are able to involve yourself with high-level professionals and other creative types. People who have seriously impressive skill sets are whom you should attempt to surround yourself with. This is a great card for those looking to give out expert advice or help others in need. If you are on the right vocational track you should find yourself amongst those who possess large reformist visions for the world. Integrating the visions of other virtuous people is always going to be one of your keys to long-term vocational success. If you can find people who are of merit and have a higher spiritual intent, then you would do well to consider teaming up with them or utilizing their services. You should have good luck finding these experts in their field and getting them on board with your mission.

The key here is to go into your vocation with an open heart, while also implementing a discerning fiscal mind. Classes in ethics and leadership are always favored with this disposition. It doesn't matter if you are giving or receiving. This is a generally altruistic expression of a vocational card so do your best to share the wealth with others around you. Remember wealth comes in many forms…material, mental, spiritual, philosophical, emotional, artistic etc. Share what you have for the best results! I would also look into youth mentorship programs, as this always seems to be a beneficial area for you as well. Careers that might be good include: accounting, consulting, venture capitalist, entrepreneur, philanthropist, crowdfunding expert, teacher, caregiver, early childhood worker, financial analyst, lawyer, researcher, chef, pilot, philosopher, life coach or guidance counselor.

Negative

This card has a bad habit of throwing good money after bad and supporting people who do not deserve your consideration long-term. Remember, if people have not proved themselves through their personal actions that you have observed first hand, you would do well to not lend them your resources. Much of your time can be taken up dealing with people who want to abuse your natural generosity. This can also be a bad card when you are born into a family that doesn't force you to go out and work for a living. You can then fit into the trust fund baby stereotype and treat people with a serious lack of appreciation. When you are suffering from this archetype you can expect things to be perpetually handed to you or you may just view everyone as somehow beneath you. Every form of life in the universe has a purpose, no matter how lowly or grotesque it may seem to you. I can assure you that if you were born on earth you aren't all that high and mighty and sooner or later the piper will come requesting payment for your actions, be they good or bad. Obviously poor people have a right to exist as well, they might just be on a different spiritual quest than yourself.

I am sure somewhere along the incarnational line you have been poor yourself, so you can't fairly judge someone based upon income alone. Heck I was poor most of my life, but yet here I am writing a book trying to help you! Am I scum? I guess that's up to you to decide! Perhaps these economically challenged folks took a vow of poverty before they entered into this life as they wanted to focus on less materialistic matters overall. There are many reasons for poverty, some of them self imposed, others are karmic in nature. Obviously there have been many spiritual saintly types who have renounced materialism of any form. Are these people also degenerates? I think not – in fact they have transcended the need for capital. These types of people deal with internal capital, as they have come to terms with the universe and understand that their needs will always be met as long as they are applying themselves towards their own personal development. This world is always based upon perspective, the more perspective we can garner for ourselves the more truth we will be given long-term.

Dates associated with this card

May 31st, June 30th, July 29th, August 28th, September 27th, October 26th, November 25th, December 24th.

> *Charity bestowed upon those who are worthy of it is like good seed sown on a good soil that yields an abundance of fruits. But alms given to those who are yet under the tyrannical yoke of the passions are like seed deposited in a*

Austin Muhs

bad soil. The passions of the receiver of the alms choke, as it were, the growth of merits.

Buddha

7 of Disks

This is a very spiritual vocational card in many ways as it tries its darndest to transcend the traditional materialist paradigm and return to nature in some way. Perhaps you are happiest in the outdoors, working on a farm, as a horticulturist, agriculturist, or participating in husbandry. Perhaps you would be much happier when focusing on a vocation that works into a slower pace of life. This type of work would allow you to pair down and live a more utilitarian lifestyle. Look into different forms of occupation which are off the beaten path, things like: divination, astrology, philosophy, color theorist, artist, sculptor, writer, blogger or journalist would be particularly helpful with this archetype, as it would free up space for you to expatiate your thoughts and may give rise to a whole new understanding of existence itself.

One of my writing teachers told me that when you write, you are able to become the god of your own imagination. I love that statement and I feel like it's a truly incredible insight into the world of imaginative passion that drives a writer to write. Being that reality isn't always what we want it to be, I feel that sometimes the freedom in our own heads is the only freedom we really have in this world. Especially if you find yourself towards the beginning stages of your career taking flak from some phony in a suit. It's hard to really appreciate life unless you feel there is some freedom to strive towards. The trick lies in understanding that external financial

The Soul System of Tarot

freedom is just another type of trap. Sure you might not have to clock in and out everyday, but you still have to get up and take action out in the world in some meaningful way, lest you suffer from your own internal soul screaming for transcendental meaning.

Negative

On the downside of this transit you may be something of a perpetual wanderer. If you fail to bring meaning from within your own life, you are forced to face countless disappointments as external reality continually fails to bring you the solace and success that you seek. Many times life just isn't exactly what we want it to be, usually it's much more difficult than we anticipate. As such, we must be prepared to go and carve our own lives out of the unforgiving stone canvas that is the world. If you are in doubt of this phenomena just take a look at the animal kingdom. Most animals barely have time to rest; they are in a perpetual state of purposeful motion the entirety of their waking lives, as they intrinsically understand the inherent value of life.

Being that we humans are also a form of animal, we need to maintain reverence for the inherent opportunities of spiritual advancement that life presents to us on a daily basis. Obviously things that are more difficult are usually more rewarding. Why does everyone like the hottest girl/guy in school? Aside from beauty or charm, it's usually a scarcity driven thing, as these types of people are usually hard to land a date with. Therefore many times the difficulty determines the value. When you mail in an effort on your own life, the value of your own life also goes down. So with this archetype, you have to really apply yourself in a way that allows you to stay in touch with your inner value system. Start becoming comfortable going your own way and leave the societal safeguards behind. Your quest will always be a bit different, so you need to come to terms with being a true individual and all that that entails. If you are unable to achieve what you are meant to during your time here, your higher self will be the one kicking you in the head later on. So don't be afraid to put in the effort, rewards will be forthcoming in time.

So in essence neither laziness nor apathy presents a viable solution or way out of your spiritual predicament. The bottom of the mountain is a good place to be if you find yourself there, as you can easily realize that there is nowhere to go but up! Take on your karma willingly, don't be frustrated by a lack of employment here and there and by all means be patient. It may take some time for you to fully express your aptitudes in vocational life, but when you do you will become an inspiration for all those around you!

Dates associated with this card

July 30th, August 29th, September 28th, October 27th, November 26th, December 25th.

> *Patience is not simply the ability to wait - it's how we behave while we're waiting.*
>
> Joyce Meyer

8 of Disks

This sign is the archetypal work card in many ways; it really allows you to thrive in any situation requiring a quick mind, an outside-the-box mindset or a cutting edge approach. This is an archetype of the leader, the organizer and the social organizer. This archetype will force you to

The Soul System of Tarot

constantly reinvent your methods, so it also requires you to learn when and how to slow down and go into a spiritual time out to re-gather your forces. The key with this card is remembering that you are only as good as your last gig. As soon as you get on your high horse and think that you are too good for your work, then you will lose the respect of those around you, along with the financial security you crave. If you respect your work, then your work will intrinsically respect you.

Many times it's hard for us to understand the long-term ramifications of our work in other peoples lives. It's not good to brag or boast, just remember that doing a good job is reward enough within itself. In terms of vocational development in the universe, remember that in this realm, someone is always watching. No efforts made sincerely with a benevolent heart will be made in vain. Good ethics and a solid commitment to a mutual victory/win for your clients and yourself is key as well. If your clients don't know that you are out there to give them 110 percent then it's hard to develop a meaningful sense of trust within your work life. Without trust and the ability to help others fulfill their dreams, work becomes a hollow bunch of game playing. You shouldn't be surprised that clients will go out of their way to see the success of your endeavors when they know that you truly care for them.

Look for unique skills that allow your project management skills or business model to stand out from the pack. Look into working with large art projects, multimedia productions, teaching, husbandry, architecture and real estate development, as these are good areas of development for you career wise. Apprenticeship in your preferred area of work is a good move for you as well. Anything creative and outside the box that involves management should be a solid go-to for you!

Austin Muhs

Negative

If you are sloppy in your work style or unable to truly connect with your clientele on a meaningful level, you will have yourself to answer to down the line. Understanding that great people put their work above their thoughts of personal gain will allow you to maintain your integrity and work ethic in all situation. It takes many years to become a master at anything, so try to enjoy the process, and don't take all of the difficulties inherent in your task to heart. Time is a great teacher and those who refuse to humble themselves to their work, will eventually be made humble by one universal force or another. Humans are not the masters of this dimension we are merely visitors here. Bookkeeping is another problem area for you if you are not careful. Perhaps a simple accounting class or trusted budgeting professional will be able to help you solve this issue. There are no shortcuts to your destiny. Remember Lao Tzu's advice: "Nature never rushes, yet everything gets accomplished".

Dates associated with this card

July 31st, August 30th, September 29th, October 28th, November 27th, December 26th.

> *A graduation ceremony is an event where the commencement speaker tells thousands of students dressed in identical caps and gowns that 'individuality' is the key to success.*
>
> *Robert Orben*

The Soul System of Tarot

9 of Disks

With this card it is very possible that in adulthood you are able to find money easily, or perhaps you had a fortunate upbringing. This is a card that on it's upside truly values wealth and appreciates the positive use of personal power it can bring to the world. For you to find a project you truly believe in is the key to your greater success. Time takes its toll on your enterprising spirit if you don't really value the greater purposes behind what it is you are doing on the day-to-day level. The risk is that money comes so easily that you don't understand the greater value behind it.

The most universally applicable wealth story here would be that of Shakyamuni Buddha who was born into royalty, but upon learning of the sufferings of the commoners' lives beyond the palace walls, took it upon himself to leave all the wealth (and his wife/child behind) and embrace a spiritual life instead. This is not to say that wealth and money are not spiritual, as much as it is trying to say that wealth and money can be a trap. For young Shakyamuni he understood that this wealth could prevent spiritual development on some levels.

Obviously, not everyone born on the 9 of disks day will find massive wealth, in fact many will go through an intense amount of inner poverty until they figure out what true wealth is based upon out in the external world. It's about a wealth of consciousness, an inner greatness that is attained only when you know that whatever activities you take part in they are helping the world to expand. People fail to realize that you are actually educating others by educating themselves. The crazy thing about us human beings is that our energetic fields are permeable, which means that people can actually learn through osmosis just from being around you. This is why many people will physically follow around true spiritual masters; this happens due to the fact that people around them can attain a certain spiritual high from that person's energy field, which attracts them like moths to a flame. Whether this form is healthy is up for debate, I'm just pointing out that the phenomenon exists.

Negative

The risk with this archetype would be that you fall into a purely materialistic viewpoint where you don't value the world overall. You could fail to appreciate the opportunities presented by your challenges during life and instead decide to shrink from the gravity of your difficulties. This course of action would result in living a routine, boring and uninspired life. Only you know how to inherently challenge yourself and embrace your spiritual quest in stride. The good news here is that no matter where you are at it's never too late to change course. I was on the wrong road during my early years for the most part. This caused me much stress and sorrow when I was striving to gain other peoples approval, make money and find the hottest girl I could find. I was running away from anything meaningful, but I eventually realized that running is more painful than facing the difficulties willingly.

You should always be able to make a new kind of life for yourself. Just remember that it's not up to the world to give you joy and happiness, you have to create those things for yourself. Many times you have to "steal" the joys of life in the dead of night. Attaining sustainable happiness in the world is an elusive thing in general and constitutes a difficult task for anyone. We are born into this world as a pack of misfits. The true joy lies in creating harmony

The Soul System of Tarot

amongst the mostly misguided souls you will encounter out there in the "real" world. Nature is always going to play a crucial part in this process, as nature is one of the few things that puts up no pretenses. Granted, I believe that evil does exist within nature, but there is also a system of eternally sustainable/regenerative life. This system has been put in place to become our eternal silent teacher. Remember you get out of life what you put in, if you are not putting good ingredients into your life then it's no wonder things are not progressing as you might have once hoped. If you're into relationships you should go find a great love life, if you are into careers, go and conquer a vocation and if you want it all, well…I wish you the best of luck!

Dates associated with this card

August 31st, September 30th, October 29th, November 28th, December 27th.

> *I grew up with the sea, and poverty for me was sumptuous; then I lost the sea and found all luxuries gray and poverty unbearable.*
>
> Albert Camus

10 of Disks

You lucky buggers…I really want you to remember how this card feels this lifetime. You have a good shot at meaningful spiritual development with this card, along with a healthy dose of vision to help build a better vision for the world. The 10 of disks rules all things visionary, grand successes, people like Stan Lee who institute total revolutions within their particular industry. These are the George Orwells, the people who make movies like *The Matrix*. Not only does this card specialize in bringing larger philanthropic motives to the masses, this card just doesn't know when to stop. When you find your passion with this card you want to pursue it until your dying breath. Finding passion might come easier for you than for others, so use that passion to inspire the world. Remember money is only healthy when it is flowing and moving. Work on larger than life dreams such as building spiritual sites or large creative institutions of one kind or another. Your overall focus could lean towards building things that promote a legacy. This can be a very entrepreneurial card that shows you multi-tasking and perhaps taking on many different roles as your vocation evolves.

Obviously if you're still in your younger years you might not have amassed much wealth just yet, but keep the faith young Skywalker. If you are persistent it will happen for you! Remember that money without a dedicated purpose behind its implementation is worthless. Without a worthwhile purpose, excess money becomes a decadent ego driven mechanism for dehumanization. I always find it easiest to work on finding yourself while forgoing the common egoistic sufferings of this world. Obviously at the end of our lives the only things we really own are the treasures of our soul, so focus on amassing those treasures and richness will follow you wherever you may roam.

Negative

It's funny, I once did a reading at an event for a very high profile law firm. All of the top attorneys/execs at that firm drew the 10 of disks reversed. This portended to their devious agendas, crime, evil,

The Soul System of Tarot

malfeasance and general lack of being able to hold anything in the world sacred. (There are many attorneys I like by the way, perhaps this firm just had some serious ethical issues!) Basically the people operating on the negative side of this card are helping to perpetuate an evil legacy. They are helping to generate negative structures out in the world that will perpetuate beyond their lifetime.

Time is a grand adventure but if we cannot discipline ourselves appropriately to use moderation when necessary then we will become a slave to our own ambitions. I love the quote from St. Augustine, "A man has as many masters as he has vices". I feel this to be supremely true. For the negative 10 of disks person, this is usually an addiction to power, control, ego and affluence. This type of person enjoys being a narcissistic puppet master as they feel that earth is the ultimate domain for this type of behavior. The negative 10 of disks could easily be a crooked politician, attorney, mob boss, gang leader or anyone with a twisted penchant for evil. Obviously evil in this dosage didn't just pop up out of the ether. Perhaps your parents had their own battles with the dark side and you absorbed their patterns or you actively decided to take after them on some level. You might just think that you have the right to manipulate life like it is your personal ball of putty. You may be a bit too narcissistic or sociopathic to ever take a look at your own life. All I can tell you is that the end result of living life in this manner never ends well. Hopefully you are able to use these masterful planning talents for the good of humanity. If not, don't worry, someone will come to enforce vengeance upon you soon enough, in this life or the next! Oh I didn't mention the perpetual paranoia inherent in this type of lifestyle, oh yeah…that comes with the program as well.

Austin Muhs

So do your best to find ways to put people to work out in society in benevolent fashion. Because while you are operating on the dark side, it's hard to say exactly where you will end up. It could be a darker dimension of some sort or perhaps you create a psychological jail cell for yourself inside your own mind! Just do yourself a favor and attempt to lead a moralistic and virtuous lifestyle so you won't have to worry these issues!

Dates associated with this card

October 30th, November 29th, December 28th.

Humility is the true key to success. Successful people lose their way at times. They often embrace and overindulge from the fruits of success. Humility halts this arrogance and self-indulging trap. Humble people share the credit and wealth, remaining focused and hungry to continue the journey of success.

Rick Pitino

Chapter 7

The 9 Card Spread

And now the moment we have all been waiting for. This is my unique take on a spread that has up until now only incorporated 9 cards...only a true rebel such as myself would put 15 cards in something called the "9 Card Spread"! I jest but still, this is my own unique amalgamation of techniques based on my experiences thus far in using Astrology, Tarot and Numerology in my private practice. This is where I will show you how you can put these archetypal cards into practice within your own personal readings. This chart uses you or your client's own archetypes to help you to get a more comprehensive picture of your own life perspective and how that will relate to the cards at hand. It has taken me years of theological study to compile this special reading which will help you to see your transformation over the next 3 to 6 months.

You will then be able to uncover your true life trajectory over the next 3 or 6 months of your life. Depending on how intensive you want to get, you can choose a different time period to look at, with shorter time periods being more descriptive than longer time periods. I personally feel that astrological charts are better if you're going to try and look at periods of time beyond the 1-year mark. This reading goes over all of the changes you will be encountering during this period of your life. It shows you who you are and who you are becoming.

At this point, if you haven't downloaded the chart you will need to do this now.

With the chart in hand, the spread is much simpler to understand. This will save you time trying to build the image in your mind. It will also help long term for memorization of the spread and it's corresponding meanings. Although knowing the form of the spread is a major key to the reading, interpretation is obviously where the magic happens, which is why you should also have downloaded Michael Tsarion's book, *The Path of the Fool,* at this juncture. Having the true definitions of the cards readily available is also essential to effective readings. Again there are free definitions online, but most of them are junk or at the very least not comprehensive.

Building the entirety of the story through usage of the cards is the way to go until you really become in touch with your intuitive side, at which point your own potential in your mind can take over a portion of the heavy lifting for you. But I will cover this more in chapter 8 as well.

The Soul System of Tarot

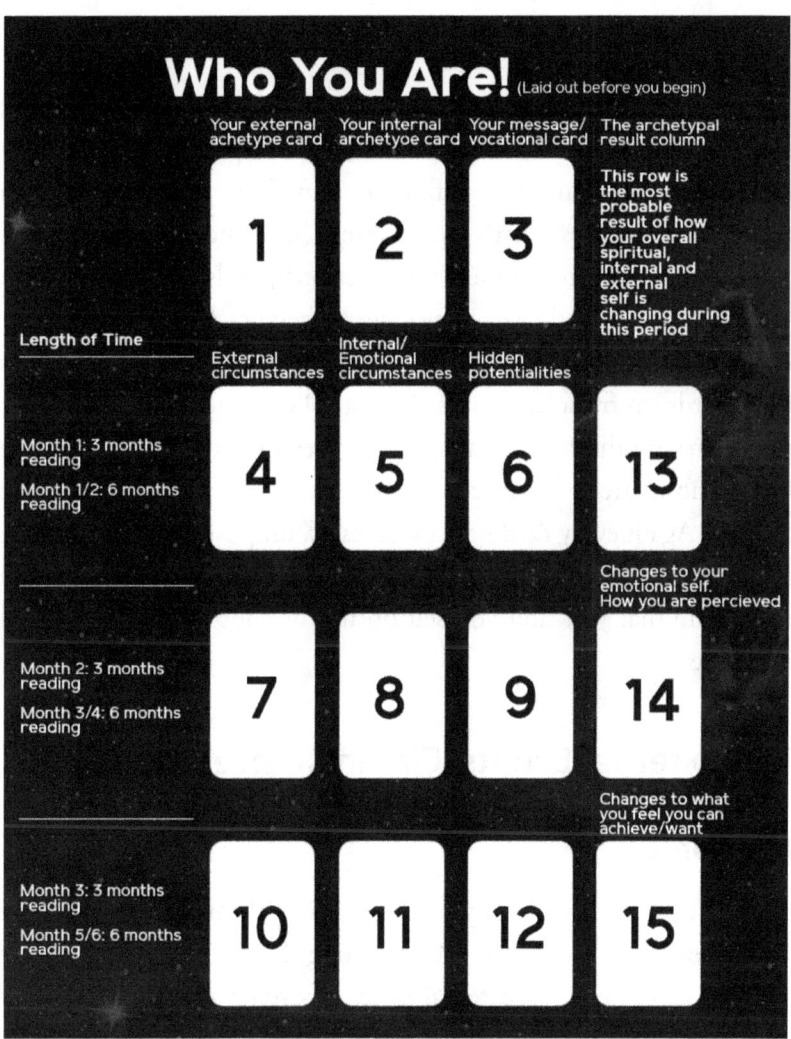

Table 1.5

Your Permanent Archetypal Cards (Top Row)

The top 3 cards (13,14 and 15 respectively) are your permanent archetypal cycle cards. These cards don't change although the way that you respond to their influences can. I go into the in-depth descriptions of these cards in Chapters 3, 4 and 5 respectively. I would advise you to look up your personal cards and meditate on how these cards and their respective archetypes have affected your life thus far. If you are doing a reading for a client I like to address these cards up front as it gives them a solid framework from which to understand their own past and how they can attain balance in the future, no matter what events they are going to face in the next lot of time. Again every card has two sides. With positive focus, anyone should be able to channel the more benevolent side of the card and make sure that you find yourself on top of your respective internal objectives.

The External Events/Circumstances Column

Position 1

This card talks about what you will be going through physically and on the external level during the coming 1-3 months. This allows you to understand the external series of events and circumstances, which will present themselves at that time. Will your attention be more focused on day-to-day career tasks? Or will you be energetically pulled away to focus more on relationships? Or will you just need to take care of odds-and-ends tasks around the home front? Will people of an unbalanced psychological status be entering your environment to throw you off kilter? Will your plans come to fruition or will a lack of planning lead you to futility's doorstep? These are the types of questions that will be answered by looking at the cards within the external column of the reading (cards 1-4-7 respectively). Remember you are not just looking up definitions you are also trying to see how the cards interrelate with the other cards in that row or column to tell a story.

Remember that we have to move beyond the linear forms of thinking when we are doing a reading as the cards on opposing ends of the reading might interrelate to tell you something. Again this is a matter of subtly developing your intuition and learning to trust the cards when they want you to look at a particular subject or in a particular direction. You can always look to the suit (i.e. swords, cups, wands etc.) to show you what form of external reality you will be dealing with most prevalently during this period. This will allow you to know if your reality will be more mentally, emotionally, physically, or emotionally focused at this time.

Position 4

This encapsulates the same attributes of the card in position 1, it just corresponds to months 2, or 3-4 depending on the length of time you are reading for.

Position 7

This encapsulates the same attributes of the card in position 1, it just corresponds to months 3, or 5-6 depending on the length of time you are reading for.

Austin Muhs

The Internal Development Column

Position 2

This card dictates your emotional temperament during the next 1-3 months. It allows you to understand your own psychological battles during this time. How will you feel about events around you? How will your baseline emotional disposition be affected? Will you be able to credibly balance your own emotional state? Will personal relationships throw you off guard? Will you jump into a poorly conceived relationship? Will you require external healing/balancing work? Will others be supportive of your internal quest to develop at this time, or will you need to shun them and go your own emotional way so to speak? Will time work for you or against you at this juncture?

Again, this card is all about how you will feel about the events taking place around you. What will your emotional disposition be like? How can you take the battles of day-to-day life and transmute them into meaningful emotional growth? How will others be responding to you emotionally? Will they be sensitive to your needs? Or will they shun you in hopes that you can take care of their needs? Will your emotional energy be high and bountiful? Or should you save your emotional energy for yourself and shun the needs of others at this time? All of these and more can be answered by looking at the internal line of cards (cards 2,5 and 8 respectively). These cards can also show psychic development as well as it rules everything governing the psyche and emotional body of the querent.

The Soul System of Tarot

Position 5

This encapsulates the same attributes of the card in position 2, it just corresponds to months 2, or 3-4 depending on the length of time you are reading for.

Position 8

This encapsulates the same attributes of the card in position 2, it just corresponds to months 3, or 5-6 depending on the length of time you are reading for.

The Hidden Developments Column

Position 3

This card represents your spiritual, otherworldly, or hidden influences that will play out unexpectedly. It is a bit of an X factor card. What are not you currently considering that will present itself during this 1-2 month period? What are your higher guides wanting you to integrate during this time? Many times we are presented with good opportunities that we pass by due to having blinders on or because we are suffering from a one-dimensional vision of how our reality could turn out. If we can have a degree of openness about our lives then things will go much smoother, as all possibilities are only open to a person who is open to all possibilities.

In a philosophical sense, we will probably never really be able to apprehend the entirety of what this world has to teach us, but we can understand everything there is to know about ourselves. As such this hidden influences line of cards, cards 3-6-9 respectively, draw us towards this more intimate knowledge of ourselves and of the circumstances that will surround us at that time. What is the deeper spiritual meaning of my life at this time? Are there any direct warnings or any unconventional advice that I need to heed at this time? Are there any particular strategies that I can implement to succeed despite the obstacles around me at the moment (cards 1-4-7 respectively)? Will you have unexpected assistance during this time? Will unseen forces come to your aid? Or will your plans be thwarted due to unrighteous intentions? Or should you reconsider your intentions or make a different plan altogether for this period? These are the types of questions you should look to answer when reading this card in the spread.

Position 6

This encapsulates the same attributes of the card in position 3, it just corresponds to months 2, or 3-4 depending on the length of time you are reading for.

Position 9

This encapsulates the same attributes of the card in position 2, it just corresponds to months 3, or 5-6 depending on the length of time you are reading for.

The Archetypal/Result Column

The cards on the right represent the larger thematic changes inherent within these cycles of transition represented by the other cards: they show the larger archetypal changes happening within the

The Soul System of Tarot

querent for better or for worse. These cards not only represent final outcomes, but also the larger archetypal changes that you are going through on a more personal subconscious level. They will help you to understand the larger themes regarding the "who, what and why" behind your own spiritual development. They also detail what you are psychologically working on becoming. Every being in the universe is aspiring to be something energetically different than what it is right now. This is because change is the only constant in the universe. Whether an individual is consciously or subconsciously aware, our deeper soul always wants us to make progress.

Existentially speaking we all die a mini death every time we go to sleep and are reborn in the morning. This accumulation of rebirths happening during our life is supposed to catapult us to newer and greater heights within our own spiritual developmental cycles. Now some people will totally ignore this type of cycle and say, "What do you mean? I am exactly the same person I was when I went to sleep last night." Well technically you are and you aren't. Do you not think that your dreams have also changed your perspective on your day-to-day habits and issues as well? I think we have all had a dream or two that scared us into some kind of change in our life. I'm sure we have all had a dream or two that also inspired us and made us realize that there are greater potentialities outside of this reality (i.e. flying dreams etc.).

Even though practically speaking, sleep hits a mini reset button within the mind to help decompress our minds. In much the same way that a computer has to defragment its disk drives periodically to keep things organized, dreams have a much greater function than that. Now do I think that sleep is the end all and be all for human development? No, but obviously it has its purpose in the human existence. I have seen and experienced some pretty incredible things while I have been asleep, as I would imagine most of you all out there have as well, so I think it's worth noting that in these archetypes we embody the mutable in our lives and our dreams reflect these subconscious changes. If we could only embody enough spiritual power to take notice, then these changes might have ever greater impacts up the human condition and upon reality itself.

Position 10

This card serves to show your results from the either month 1, or month 1-2 depending on the timetable of your inquiry. This card represents the most probably outcome of your efforts. What will the final result be? What are you learning about during this cycle overall? What is the base level lesson for you during this period? What type of person are you trying to embody or become during said period? Is there an overt warning with regards to your behavior during said period or can you continue unobstructed? What type of archetype is the querent moving towards? Is this a good thing or a bad thing? Are we able to truly make the changes that we want in our life, or are we expecting too much too soon out of a given period? Do we need to reign in our ambition or ramp it up? Is change good for this period, or should we sit back and contemplate. This card serves to show us the overarching end-result of our effort during any given period.

Position 11

This card serves to show your results from the either month 2, or month 3-4 depending on the timetable of your inquiry. What will the final result be? What are you learning about during this cycle overall? What is the base level lesson for you during this period? What type of person are you trying to embody or become during said period? Is there an overt warning with regards to your behavior during said period or can you continue unobstructed? What type of archetype is the querent moving towards? Is this a good thing or a bad thing? Are we able to truly make the changes that we want in our life, or are we expecting too much too soon out of a given period? Do we need to reign in our ambition or ramp it up? Is change good for this period, or should we sit back and contemplate? This card serves to show us the overarching end-result of our effort during any given period.

Position 12

This card serves to show your results from the either month 3, or month 4-6 depending on the timetable of your inquiry. What will the final result be? What are you learning about during this cycle overall? What is the base level lesson for you during this period? What type of person are you trying to embody or become during said period? Is there an overt warning with regards to your behavior during said period or can you continue unobstructed? What type of archetype is the querent moving towards? Is this a good thing or a bad thing? Are we able to truly make the changes that we want in our life, or are we expecting too much too soon out of a given period? Do we need to reign in our ambition or ramp it up? Is change good for this period, or should we sit back and contemplate? This card serves to show us the overarching end-result of our effort during any given period.

Chapter 8

How to Use the Cards to tell a Story

When you are reading the cards you should always keep in mind that it is the space between the notes, which allows the music to happen. If you do this for long enough you start to recognize patterns and the characters residing within the Tarot will begin to speak with you. If you step back and allow the symbols to speak to you, then you can really become very skilled very quickly, but when you when you bring preconceived baggage of how you think the Tarot should advise us, then we will quickly be humbled by the truth of coming events in reality.

The Tarot will always give you enough rope to hang yourself, even though its ultimate goal is to teach you, it has no problem offering fair warnings for misguided egoistic behavior. Nor does it have a problem warning you about said behavior in others either. Allow the symbols to be your teacher them and embody them as you would accept a lesson from a respected professor or mentor. The symbols are generally neutral, so there is nothing to fear. When you understand something thoroughly it can take much of the fear out of the exercise. Think about it, when you understand how to take a written test in school it becomes less nerve-racking, but I bet everyone got a bit nervous when they found out that they would have to take such a test in the beginning. Most everyone has a fear of the unknown, so that being said, learning to jump willingly into such unknown subjects takes a bit of courage, as it is like arranging a meeting with your long lost parent.

The symbols existing within the Tarot are indestructible, and eternal (at least as far as I can gather) they will be around as long as there is a civilization of some sort to support their conscious existence. When a Tarot reading is administered properly, it becomes a mentor, a best friend, a teacher, a confidant, a prophet and a storyteller. If you look at the cards as separate in and unto themselves then you will be missing the point of the exercise. The Tarot in its entirety represents a large cast of characters that are prominent within the play of life. Foreknowledge that these different players, pawns and obstacles exist will prevent them from getting the best of you down the line. Before you attack your enemy (internal or external) you must study their every movement. This kind of detective activity is exactly what the Tarot allows us to practice. When we sharpen our wits and hone our intuitive discernment then there will be few things in life that can get the best of us. Knowing the future helps us to brace our spiritual and emotional bodies for the shock that occurs when life ends up being something vastly different than anything we ever thought that it would be. At least in my experience, life always seems to be able to surprise me.

So enough blathering about all of that, by now you are probably wondering how do you tell a story using the cards? Well the key is to really understand each of the cards like you would understand one of your good friends. The key to this you ask? The key is to practice, practice, practice! You should not only practice doing

THE SOUL SYSTEM OF TAROT

readings, but more importantly you should work to thoroughly memorize the definitions laid out in *The Path of the Fool* by Michael Tsarion which I highly suggest you invest in.

So for example, when looking at how to tell a story you first need to evaluate the characters involved in the plot. Let's say that you put some of your ultra conservative friends and a few of your hedonist party friends in one room – that would make for a very awkward and difficult social setting right? There may be a conflict involved due to the differing lifestyles and points of view, heck there may even be a shouting match that evening, who knows, right? Well the same can be said for the cards, depending upon the cast of characters that you have appear in your reading you can start to imagine how that party (reading) will end up playing out. Well Johnny got too drunk and started hitting on Sally, Sally got mad and told Jill, who actually liked Johnny and then started to dislike Sally because Johnny liked Sally instead of her, etc. These types of human dramas start to pop out at you when you're doing a reading. Depending on the client you can come back with many different types of readings. On the other side of the spectrum, you will also experience readings that are almost 100 percent internally based. Readings that talk about what is going on inside that person's head and how they can best cope or communicate with the feelings associated with said period. Again there are infinite numbers of combinations that can come up in a given reading so that's why practice is so necessary. Until you understand how the cards interact with one another on a psychological level you will be stuck on the surface level of the reading.

You can also have difficult readings, when most of the cards you pull are largely associated with "negative" attributes. Now this may be upsetting to your client or yourself, but I can assure you that this is no reason to fear. We all have periods of danger and difficulty in our life. These periods can actually be some of the most rewarding in all of life, so if your client starts to whine or squirm remind them that these are the times that define who you really are. People don't generally discover their true selves until the chips are down in one-way or another.

I think we have all had a difficult situation within our life in which we were forced to play to a hostile crowd in one form or another. This can happen in a reading as well. Say you have an eager young businessman excited about starting his new hot dog stand, but what he doesn't know is that he has decided to start his new stand next to hostile gang territory. If you can start to look at these aforementioned scenarios with an open mind and a keen sense of observation you can save yourself a good deal of stress. The cards are always working overtime to try and help you understand the hidden subconscious story, which is what really drives external events. Anything that happens in the external world originates from an internal world of psychic potentialities. This is the world we need to start to decode.

Miscellaneous advice on doing readings...

You should always remember that the cards are meant to be a training wheels type of device, not a crutch. When you are overly reliant upon the method of divination instead of your own intrinsic intuition or your own inherent sense of right and wrong, you can be defeating the point of the exercise. On one level you should be working towards not needing the cards. The cards are just helping to show us the invisible channels of energy operating behind our current incarnation of reality. In time, you will begin to recognize these channels of energy as you internalize the wisdom within the cards. The cards will teach you and eventually they might just become a part of you. The cards can become a trusted friend and ally. Like any good friend, when they are not there in person, it can be just as valuable to carry them with you in spirit. Their lessons will follow you around like a warm blanket, imbuing you with warmth that you can then impart to others. Now I think that many readers will eventually get to a point where they don't need the cards at all, but I am not going to comment further here because I think that everyone is at a different level in this regard.

When doing readings for others, it is actually good to use the cards even if you don't need them because it shows the client firsthand that they picked out those specific energies, it therefore puts the blame squarely on the cards if warnings or any unsettling news is presented. Plus, many people are visual and respond to the imagery in the cards. You will commonly find that clients can get sassy or try to project their psychological baggage on you if you're giving them bad news. Luckily the cards are a good buffer for this common defense mechanism. They allow you an easy rebuttal against any of your clients' defense mechanisms, as you can say, "Look, you picked the cards, I'm just reading them!" I think this is invaluable, especially with people who are naturally skeptical of intuitive individuals. Let the cards become your arbiter for truth. Remind them in a comical way of what the cheese-ball infomercial psychic Ms. Cleo said, because "The cards don't lie..." You can also let them know that if a reader is doing his or her job right, the querent (client) is just having a deep conversation with himself or herself. The reader should just serve as an interpreter for the client's subconscious while explaining the meanings on the cards!

Possible questions to ask while doing readings

1. What will my outcome look like if I pursue this path, person, objective, social endeavor, night out etc. ?
2. How can I best utilize my time over the coming months?
3. How is _____ person responding to me?
4. What is _____ person struggling with right now that is causing them to act a certain way?
5. Is this advisor, gadget, vacation, degree etc. worth the money I am going to invest in it?
6. How can I best pursue my own emotional/spiritual growth over the coming months?
7. Is this relationship in my highest spiritual good?
8. What are the main themes of the year going to be for me?
9. Sometimes you can also do readings for different types of food to see how they will affect your body. You may be surprised at what you find out here.
10. Would an alternative healing modality benefit me at this time?
11. Is this person/project worth my time/resources?
12. Will the energetic field be safe for me or toxic to me if I go to this certain place/event?

The Soul System of Tarot

13. How do I go about learning more about myself at the current time?

Which Tarot Deck Should I Use?

Well Mr. Tsarion points out that the most historically accurate and symbolically powerful two decks available are the Rider-Waite deck and Thoth decks. The Rider Waite deck is the most universally used overall and contains the most iconic imagery people associate with the Tarot. The Thoth deck was created by The Order of the Golden Dawn and A.E. Waite created the Rider Waite around the turn of the century.

Each of these decks was comprised after compiling over twenty-five years of occult research by each of their respective creators. Even though the OTO/Golden Dawn can appear to be a spurious organization, that shouldn't color your viewpoint on lady Frieda Harris' lifes work. It's hard to imagine that a more beautiful thing could have ever come into existence with regards to sheer imagination surrounding the mystical Tarot. She truly poured her soul into the imagery to effectively capture that 25 plus years of research in a meaningful way.

So go ahead and say what you will about the practitioners, (obviously there were some issues with those folks) but the deck itself is sound! Basically these guys constituted an encyclopedic counsel on esoteric information and they threw everything they had into these decks.

Until Mr. Waite restored the deck back to its primordial state in the early 1900's, the symbolism within the Tarot decks of that time had fallen into a state of utter disrepair. The "professional" Tarot readers prominent in France and other areas of Europe had incorporated numerous erroneous and ill-informed symbols into their versions of the Tarot. These less powerful decks had become commonplace from the 1600s to the late 1800's. It took these two brilliant esoteric scholars to come along and reinstate this powerful tool of psychological healing. So if you want my advice these are the 2 best decks to get. But if you are dead set on being a new age reader and want to get an "Angel Deck" so be it! Just don't come crying to me when your job is that much harder because the angel deck comprises a less than accurate compendium of the full range of human experiences.

Truth be told, everything has some divinatory ability. Because simply put, we all possess a subconscious as far as I am aware. Flipping a coin is perhaps the simplest form of divination, but I find that if utilized with a pure intent, flipping a coin can even be a powerful tool from time to time. This of course isn't the best thing to use, but in a pinch it's possible to get a quick second opinion on matters. I am bringing this up because I want to relay the fact that I'm sure some readers use these other "Tarot decks" with some degree of success. Yet for me personally, I want the best tools possible to assist my clients and myself alike. It's like a professional guitarist going on stage with a $50 dollar Fisher Price guitar and trying to deliver his best work – it's just not going to happen. If you want to be a pro, you would do well to befriend the Tarot decks of pros, in my humble opinion!

Without the proper symbolic archetypes in place, decks lose their spiritual compass and become less cosmically attuned to the specific factors of earth's complex time-space reality! Perhaps in other dimensions the old angel Tarot does a bang up job, but the last time I looked around, I saw more tools than angels around this joint!

The Soul System of Tarot

Watch out for Disreputable Readers!

The disreputable readers in this line of psychological healing work are a dime a dozen. You can find them in any city or state and they are a very familiar group to practitioners within the Tarot community. Heck, they make up most of the Tarot community. Disreputable readers have been "using" the Tarot as a profession since the Middle Ages in Europe, essentially becoming full time fortunetellers. I guess I should stop here and say that I don't like the term psychic, as it implies that the Tarot practitioner is telling you something that you don't already know on a deep level. As I have stated previously the role of the Tarot reader is to be a vehicle for your clients so that they are able to have an in-depth conversation with their own subconscious and/or their higher self.

I would be extremely wary of getting a reading, or any healing whatsoever from small corner Tarot shops. Now, in their defense I am sure there are a few good small corner shops out there, I just have never encountered one. I would look on Yelp or another reputable service or go by referral only if looking for a moralistic practitioner of the divination arts. For some reason these corner shops attract the bottom of the barrel with regards to the Tarot community, so be careful! It's always best to do your own readings if you are in doubt. I have routinely had clients lose thousands of dollars while listening to the advice of people operating out of these locations. There have even been cases of people losing upwards of $20,000, all in the name of receiving so-called "healing work". I have had clients purchase Cartier watches, cars and more, all because the "fortuneteller" said if they performed said fiscal transaction then they could help them somehow. The usual story you get involves a promise of the fortuneteller in the name of helping people to improve their fate, find their soul mate, remove a curse, remove an evil spirit, get rid of disease, attract more money etc. The sad part is that most people actually do have energy problems or mild health problems to one degree or another, but these shops are in no way qualified to handle any of the more difficult energetic issues in my opinion. That's assuming that they are trying to help in the first place, which is a big IF!

People with these types of issues need to find high-level acupuncturists or dedicated alternative holistic healers to address these types of problems. Without a solid foundation of morality, no healer will be that effective. Being a healer is a gift bestowed by the heavens and it's not bestowed upon the morally derelict members of humanity who whore out for a few bucks. Not to say that healers should not get paid, as they definitely should, but they need to charge for their healing services in a way that is straightforward and not manipulative. I would say that you should always use your intuition when you meet anyone new, figure out how your body feels when you are around this new person. Are you feeling queasy, do you feel light and ready to conquer the world, or do you feel like a creeper has entered your bubble. These corner shop healers pray upon the mentally distressed, emotionally disturbed and lost souls who are looking for answers in their life.

I have yet to hear a success story from a person who said that a corner shop Tarot reader had solved all of their problems. Many of these shops will include signs claiming to offer crystal or chakra healing and they may try to get you to give them money to buy materials for their "healing work".

The truth is this. I have met dozens and dozens of alternative healers and the ones that are the best at their craft have spent a

The Soul System of Tarot

lifetime becoming competent in their particular trade or field of study. It takes lots of dedication and goodwill towards humanity to become a great healer. Healing work is a very difficult profession as you end up bearing the burden of the large amounts of unhealthy energy coming from a sickly clientele. This is something you have to train for years to be able to do safely. You also need a high ethical compass to be protected in my opinion as well. All I can really tell you is that I love the Tarot dearly for helping to save me from my own self delusion, so when I see people using it unethically it makes me very angry. And as of yet I haven't seen anyone else sounding the alarm on this particular phenomenon in the industry.

Chapter 9

Every New Beginning

I feel that Michael Tsarion makes a great point about the meaning of life – life only has the meaning that we give it. I grapple everyday to recreate that meaning as, sometimes in life, what you thought your eternal quest was supposed to encapsulate ends up being a wayward destination, instead of a final one. We can never really be sure of this reality, as it is designed to keep us guessing and eternally curious. The key point I believe is just starting to get into the ring. If we don't take the field of battle, how will we ever know what we are capable of? We all know that this place can be hell and I guess for some people it can be heaven as well.

The bottom line is that our internal life is what we make it. The external world will always present us with things that need fixing or adjustment, but the internal sense of self is something that we can stabilize over time with a persistent effort at grasping and integrating the spiritual truths that we find self evident over our time being alive. If we don't learn from our lessons, then why bother to bear the weight of this suffering in the first place. We obviously choose our suffering willingly in an effort to get better on some level or we would not ended up here. Instead we could have incarnated as a dust mite, or a tree or any of the billions of other creations in the world. Obviously we wanted to master the psychologically angst so ubiquitous in the human race. So try to face the fact that you signed up for this mission and you're getting what you paid for.

The wisdom garnered through doing readings will help you to gain acceptance and self-knowledge during your quest, but you are the one responsible for pulling the deeper meanings from within your own life. You must also sift through the fractured souls on the earth at this time, so as not to be waylaid on your journey. You may feel alone, you might feel pain from being different, you may wish things were different, but I can assure you that all of these odd feeling will pass given enough time. Time and spiritual understanding do truly heal all wounds. Nature wants you to be a whole self and wants you to evolve. Whereas, the rest of the people you know may have differing opinions on that topic. Remember that your greatest undisputed allies in my view are nature and the internal voice within. Those are the two things that will never lead you astray. You will obviously receive some great teachers in your lifetime as well that will assist you, but you must first understand yourself a bit, before any great teacher will spend their valuable time with you.

No matter where you stand right now in your personal spiritual quest, I think there is always further to go on our quest towards personal development. Would the Dao, God or the universe create creation with an end goal in mind? At some point in time where every being will live in a fairy tale land somehow? Will we awaken to find demons and angels living in harmony? Will the heavens expand out to encapsulate all beings? Or are we just fooling ourselves? I would imagine that creation does go on forever and that we are supposed to just keep on ascending or transmuting this reality somehow to create ever evolving types of quests and the like.

The Soul System of Tarot

These questions are all above my pay grade so to speak, but I think they are important questions for the future of humanity and our souls in general. What is the point of humanity and where are we all headed? Will we be able to escape this world or are we supposed to reform it? It is my understanding that we can't really fix this dimension as according to Lao Tzu it is already perfected to perform the dimensional duty it was designed for. As such we must personally evolve to find out where our souls may travel to next! However you look at this world I think it's important to remember that one thing we can always work towards is our own personal reformation. And that is an option that is our birthright in this plane of existence.

I sincerely thank you all for reading and I wish you all the best of luck on your continued spiritual journey, wherever that may take you. Life isn't easy, but with persistence it can be intensely meaningful, which I believe can make up for some of our pain. Pain with purpose is never really wasted in my estimation.

Please feel free to contact me directly at www.astrologybyaustin.com for a reading or email me at neonskyrecords@gmail.com.

Be seeing you soon!

Austin Muhs

About the Author

Austin is an experienced Author, Astrologer, Numerologist and veteran Tarot Card Reader. His previous written works deal with the philosophical implications of modern economic theory, another subject near to his heart. He has also studied the occult sciences over the past seven years through the works of the theological giants in their respective fields. Austin's spiritual quest began at the age of 19 when his father died. This tremendous loss filled him with grief and led him down a negative land self-destructive life path. After immersing himself in the way of Psychology, Philosophy and Spirituality he discovered Meditation and the Hermetic Arts and was guided out of the darkness that had befallen him. He realized that the only way to make life a rich, rewarding adventure was to help others. Astrology, Tarot, and Numerology offered him a new avenue that enriched his quest of making a positive difference in other people's lives. This holistic approach gave him a thirst for self-improvement and led him to become a Tai Chi and Chi Gong practitioner; further ensconcing his deep love for nature.

Austin serves his clients throughout the beach cities of Santa Monica, Venice and Redondo Beach as well as the entire Los Angeles metropolitan area. To make an appointment with Austin please call him at 310-923-8959 or send him an email at neonskyrecords@gmail.com. Austin also works with clients worldwide via Skype.

www.ingramcontent.com/pod-product-compliance
Lightning Source LLC
Chambersburg PA
CBHW062207080426
42734CB00010B/1834